TOUCHSTONE

ETHICS AND PROFITS

The Crisis of Confidence in American Business

Leonard Silk and David Vogel

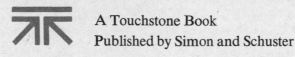

A Touchstone Book
Published by Simon and Schuster

A Touchstone Book
Published by Simon and Schuster
A Division of Gulf & Western Corporation
Simon & Schuster Building
Rockefeller Center
1230 Avenue of the Americas
New York, New York 10020
TOUCHSTONE and colophon are trademarks
of Simon & Schuster

Designed by Irving Perkins
Manufactured in the United States of America

3   4   5   6   7   8   9   10   11   12

Library of Congress Cataloging in Publication Data

Silk, Leonard Solomon, date.
  Ethics and profits
  Includes bibliographical references.
    1. Industry—social aspects—United States.
2. Business ethics   I.   Vogel, David, 1947–
joint author.   II.   Title.
HD60.5.U5S54   658.4'08   76-14461

ISBN 0-671-22343-7
ISBN 0-671-23024-7 Pbk.

Contents

5

Foreword

BUSINESSMEN are generally regarded by most people as powerful and privileged. Many businessmen, however, see themselves as politically impotent and beleaguered. Men who feel self-assured in dealing with the ordinary problems of business are often insecure when confronted with voluble special-interest groups, burgeoning governmental regulation, and the new "open society." They are painfully adjusting to a whole new set of demands, responsibilities and work situations for which neither their education nor previous work experience has adequately prepared them. The immediate origins of their present difficulties lie in the social revolution of the 1960's and 1970's. While sociologists will be arguing for years about the underlying roots of this social revolution, the effects of some of the changes on corporations and their leaders are becoming increasingly clear.

In the postwar period, American affluence grew so abundantly that many people became no longer concerned with fulfilling their basic material needs or desires, but began giving increased attention to their psychic needs. The desire to avoid the Vietnam draft induced numerous young men who had little interest in further learning to go to college, and affluence permitted many more young people to go on to advanced studies. They were not worried about later employment, perhaps because graduates were being wooed so assiduously by industry and government, and because our social welfare programs had become so widespread that even if their parents could not or would not support them, they felt sure society would. The massive influx of students, the normal radicalism of youth, the permissiveness of colleges, the corrosiveness of the Vietnam conflict, and the advent of drug subcultures led to serious campus unrest, a widespread rejection of traditional values, and a stubborn challenge to authority. The resultant distrust of all institutions (collectively labeled "the establishment") and the disdain for traditional standards of behavior spread first to noncampus youth, then to post-university liberal elements, and eventually to society as a whole. This social revolution not only manifested itself in changing value systems, but it also brought new attitudes toward work and altered ethical and social behavior throughout society. In offices and factories, workers who previously had been docile were now seeking greater involvement in the decisions affecting their work, and were demanding more satisfying work experiences.

At the time all of this was taking place, population continued to shift from rural to urban areas—especially poor blacks from the South to large northern cities. Frustrated by their unpreparedness to live and work in urban situations, underemployed because of lack of education and opportunity, and incited to unrest by the affluence around them, the urban poor also rebelled against society.

When these waves of social unrest crested, all of American society was in ferment with a social revolution that seriously affected business. Concern for the quality of life manifested itself in intense preoccupation with the environment. Special-interest groups challenged business on air and water pollution, and on protection for the ecology of even remote and uninhabited areas. Atomic energy and other forms of power generation became special targets. Politicians vied with one another to offer the most stringent legislation to prevent commercial activity from damaging the environment. The Club of Rome's first report on *Limits to Growth* set off another wave of popular concern—this time over resource use.

Protecting the consumer against not only the carelessness or callousness of business but also against his own folly was another outgrowth of the growing concern over the quality of life, abetted by a spreading distrust of business. Another by-product was the creation of the Occupational Safety and Health Administration, which tightened safety procedures in industry to a point some businessmen consider to be unreasonable. The need to help urban minorities to improve their condition led to Equal Employment Opportunity legislation, which has resulted in some reverse discrimination in order to accelerate the integration of minority groups into all levels of business.

Most businessmen were not well prepared to cope with these and other new demands society was placing on them and their enterprises. Even those who had been professionally trained in business schools often felt inadequate in dealing with special-interest groups, hostile media, anti-business government officials, and the new work force. They have been making what has been for some a most difficult transition in their fundamental philosophy and management style. They are really seeking a new philosophical base for, and another operational approach to, the new realities that confront their companies.

Since its founding, The Conference Board has held small, off-the-record meetings of business leaders that afford a unique opportunity for senior executives to exchange candid views on subjects of their own choice in peer groups. Because so many business leaders were struggling to find philosophical and operational answers to fit the new social environment, it was decided that eight of these meetings, each lasting three days, would be devoted to the question of the past, present and future social responsibilities of business. These meetings took place between September 1974 and September 1975. Some 360 executives, in groups that ranged from 35 to 55 in number, provided a fair cross-section of the country's business-leadership group. Almost every region of the nation was represented, as was almost every major type of business endeavor. As has been customary during these meetings, the discussions were enriched by a sprinkling of lawmakers, academicians and military men.

With Watergate and the post-Watergate revelations of corruption prominent in the news during these meetings, there was much soul-searching and some agonizing, because most business leaders were obviously embarrassed and angered by the shadow these events cast over business in general. Although weakness and venality beset some in all walks of life (and many businessmen honestly believe that they are as moral as any other group in society), the adverse reflection was particularly discouraging because business was already suffering a serious loss of public confidence as a result of the recession and a widespread distrust of all institutions. Much time and thought were therefore given to the ethics of business.

The growing tendency of people to look to business to meet the rising tide of expectations unleashed by the postwar boom and the Great Society programs prompted lengthy discussions of the relative roles of government and business in setting and meeting social goals. Many businessmen are appalled to find their companies called upon to tackle problems that are outside their sphere of accustomed competence and beyond their resources. Since this is a condition that is not likely to abate in the foreseeable future, the views on the subject encapsulated in this book have particular relevance to today's business leaders.

Today's business leaders—their characteristics and attitudes—would have been most surprising and interesting to the founding fathers of our country or of The Conference Board in its early days, if they could have observed these meetings. Management in America has come a long way from the merchant and farmer classes of Revolutionary days and power brokers who dominated the industrial scene when the Board first took shape in the early 1900's.

Unfortunately, too many social observers and critics still think in terms of the stereotyped characters and deeds of the so-called "robber barons," rather than focusing on the socially sensitive, highly professional managers who dominate American business life today. Involved in the discussions that underlie this book were men whose strong conservative bent has only reluctantly been modified by the new social realities. But they were as few in number as were those of such liberal tendencies that they put social goals ahead of the economic objectives of business. The overwhelming majority held the view that the prime goal of business is still to provide people with desired goods and services (and that to continue doing so requires operating profitably). But they believe that this must be done with attention to the social objectives of the public and within the restraints society has imposed. Nor is this a reluctant or even passive attitude for many. They believe businessmen as a group, endowed with resources and a capacity to get things done, must take a leadership role in setting and fulfilling social goals.

Many books have been written by academics and social critics on the social responsibility of business, but none reflects the thinking of a broad segment of the business community on this important issue. To capture contemporary business thinking on this and related problems and to present it to the public, we asked Leonard Silk, economist and member of the editorial board of *The New York Times*, and David Vogel, member of the faculty of the University of California, Berkeley, to join these meetings as objective observers and to write a book based not just on what they heard, but including their own analyses of the meaning and impact of the discussions. They were given complete freedom to write what they wished, the only restriction being that they treat all remarks as anonymous so as to protect the confidentiality of the meetings. This produced extraordinary candor in the discussions. While the selection of material used by Messrs. Silk and Vogel and the conclusions drawn are their own, I wish to compliment them on producing a perceptive and thought-provoking work.

The role of business in society has been a recurrent theme in The Conference Board's conferences and research since its inception in 1916. The relationship between private enterprise and public interest, especially as the latter is represented by the federal government, was a matter of much concern to the business leaders who founded the Board. Concern with the well-being of industrial employees was manifested in early years by pioneering studies of industrial safety and hygiene, and by a sequence of studies of the human side of business that today focus on such contemporary questions as equal-employment opportunity and job enrichment. The Board has also led the way in the study of corporate philanthropy, aid to education, and community service. It was this heritage that induced the Board to direct the attention of this series of high-level conferences to an exploration of the social concerns and ethical thinking of business as its contribution to the Bicentennial Year and also to mark its own sixtieth year.

I wish to acknowledge the leadership and dedication given to this project by G. Clark Thompson, Senior Vice President of The Conference Board, and by Lillian W. Kay, Manager, Editorial Services, who provided very valuable editorial assistance. Our greatest vote of thanks goes to the business executives and other leaders who participated in these meetings and gave extensive thought and analysis to the issues raised. Our hope is that not only they, but also the many citizens who are less intimately connected with the responsibilities of business leadership, will gain from this a better understanding of both the workings and the motivations that underlie the dynamic American economic system.

March 1976   ALEXANDER B. TROWBRIDGE, *President*
                The Conference Board

ETHICS AND PROFITS

CHAPTER ONE

Introduction: A Crisis of Confidence

IN THE EARLY and middle nineteen-seventies, a series of events shook public confidence in the American business community.

Watergate

The most dramatic of these events was Watergate—the symbol of the political and financial scandals that led to the resignation of President Nixon. Many companies, including some of the most prominent, had made illegal contributions to the Nixon campaign. By early 1976, the Watergate Special Prosecutor's Office had successfully prosecuted eighteen companies for violations of the campaign finance laws. The Securities and Exchange Commission had sued nine companies for their failure to disclose the existence of political slush funds here and abroad, and the chairman of the SEC revealed that thirty other major American corporations were under investigation for alleged bribery, kickbacks, and illegal campaign contributions. Public resentment was commonly generalized from the particular companies involved to the

17

business community as a whole—and the failure of business leaders to speak out publicly against those corporations that had engaged in illegal acts led much of the public to conclude that "they are all in this together." The public's hostile attitude toward businessmen who engaged in "white collar crime" was doubtless intensified by an awareness of business's close links with a President who had crusaded for "law and order" but had circumvented the law for his own political purposes. At the same time, many critics of business saw its illegal political behavior as an effort to circumvent the democratic political process because it was disrespected and because businessmen felt that they could protect or advance their companies' interest by buying political influence.

The Oil Explosion

A second major development that heightened public hostility toward American business was the "energy crisis," which erupted with the Arab oil embargo of late 1973 and early 1974. The chaotic conditions of fuel supply, the interminable waits, and the battles at the gasoline pumps in some parts of the country were shocking to a society utterly dependent on oil and gasoline. The soaring of oil prices and oil profits intensified public antipathy toward the oil companies. Justly or unjustly, many American accused them of "profiteering" from the supply conditions created by the Arab embargo. American businessmen, and not only those in the oil industry, cannot seem to grasp the distinction in the public mind between "legitimate profits" and "profiteering," which crucially affects attitudes toward business behavior. As Daniel

Yankelovich, a leading public-opinion analyst, told a group of business people at The Conference Board on January 15, 1976:

> Businessmen and economists do not distinguish between profit making and profiteering, but the public does. This is the distinction that Irving Kristol has made a number of times, and I think it is a well-made point. We have found, time and again, that people are not resentful of large profits if they are perceived as the result of rendering a real service. On the other hand, they are very resentful of even small profits if they think of those small profits as being made because you have your hand in the consumer's pocket. The recent oil embargo was probably the classic instance of people seeing this as a case of very large profits made not for rendering a service but, in effect, for exploiting a situation. Right or wrong, that was the perception. It has been the perception every time there has been a Populist explosion, as in the 1890's.

Foreign and Domestic Corruption

The American public in 1975 learned that United States-based corporations were involved in large-scale political gifts (some of them legal) all over the world. Exxon admitted that it had paid $46 million to Italian political parties—including $86,000 to the Italian Communist party. Many other American companies made similar "apolitical" contributions to foreign politicians in exchange for business and legislative favors. Some American companies overseas engaged in out-and-out bribery, rather than ethically questionable but legal acts. Northrop admitted it had paid off Saudi Arabian generals and other foreign officers to increase aircraft sales. Lockheed conceded that it had made big payments abroad in connection with sales of its TriStar transports, which its chairman preferred to call "kickbacks," not "bribes." Gulf Oil admitted it had yielded to political extortion in South Korea and made questionable payments elsewhere, and its chairman and two of its top officers were forced to resign.

There was a seemingly endless stream of newspaper stories that added to public cynicism about business behavior at home as well as abroad: scandals over false weighting of grains being loaded for export on the docks of New Orleans, bribery for an air route to the Bahamas, payments by fruit companies to politicians in Honduras and Guatemala, bribery to get a telephone rate increase in Alabama, payoffs to politicians for building-construction contracts in Maryland, and the continuing disclosure of political payoffs by milk producers to get price increases. Senator Charles Percy of Illinois, once president of Bell & Howell, said, "Corporate corruption, playing even the minuscule role that it does, is the dry rot of capitalism." But other observers felt that the problem of business corruption was not minuscule—and that its root cause was a poorly ordered relationship between business and government in the "mixed economy."

Inflation and Recession

As bad as the impact of business corruption on the public might have been in normal times, public hostility toward business was greatly intensified by the rapid inflation and then the deep slump of 1973–75—the worst recession in over four decades. Again, whether fairly or unfairly, consciously or unconsciously, the American public holds American business responsible for what goes wrong in the economy. And, with inflation moving up to rates as high as 14 percent per annum and unemployment at 9 percent and threatening to remain abnormally high for months and even years to come, much of the American public felt that business was failing the primary test of its competence and legitimacy—the provision of jobs and reasonably stable incomes. Thus "stagflation"—the combination of inflation and stagnation—intensified an anti-business mood the like of which had not been seen since the Depression of the nineteen-thirties.

The Public Mood

The public-opinion polls have left no room for doubt about the decline of public confidence in business. The Harris poll reported that 55 percent of the public in 1966 had expressed "a great deal of confidence" in the heads of large corporations but that this proportion had fallen to 29 percent in 1973, to 21 percent in 1974, and to 15 percent in 1975. The Yankelovich survey reported that the proportion of the public that thought "business strikes a fair balance between profits and the public interest" had dropped from 70 percent in 1968 to 20 percent by 1974. And a Gallup poll in July 1975 found that, among all institutions comprising what it called "the United States power structure," big business came in last, with a "confidence" score of 34 percent compared with 38 percent for organized labor, 40 percent for Congress, 49 percent for the Supreme Court, 52 percent for the executive branch, 58 percent for the military, 67 percent for education, and 68 percent for organized religion.

Interestingly enough, the Vietnam war appears to have had little to do with the fall of public confidence in American business; only the radicals, with their theories of the link between capitalism, imperialism, and war, blamed business for Vietnam.

Rather, it was government—the "best and the brightest" political leaders, the military, and the intelligence community —that was the principal focus of political criticism for Vietnam. To be sure, there were exceptions in business, such as Dow Chemical, with its specific link to the Vietnam war through its manufacture of napalm. Dow's public-relations director said its record of being attacked—with over two hundred major campus demonstrations against it between 1966 and 1970—was unmatched by demonstrations against recruiters of the U.S. Armed Forces, against the CIA, or against any other company. But for the most part, during the upheavals of the 1960's, business was not so much challenged as ignored, except by a relatively limited number of radicals of the left.

The 1970's are another story. The issues that have headlined political controversy in recent years—the struggle to preserve the environment, the integrity of the Presidency and the electoral process, and, perhaps most seriously, growing public anxiety about economic instability, inflation, unemployment, questions about the adequacy of energy and other resources, and of the ability of future economic growth to satisfy national needs and aspirations—all these issues go to the heart of public concern over the role and performance of business corporations in American society, and indeed throughout the world, with growing public awareness of the multinational involvement of corporations today.

While the challenge to the performance and legitimacy of the great corporations is comparable to that which business faced during the nineteen-thirties, the economic crisis of the 1970's is basically different from the Great Depression, which was a catastrophe of mass unemployment and systemic breakdown.

The Great Depression lasted so long in part because of a failure of governments to understand the necessity of creating enough monetary demand to call forth the goods that the men and machines of society were capable of producing. It was ended by the enormous increase of government expenditures to pay for World War II. But the current crisis stems not from a deficiency of demand (indeed, the universal problem is inflation) but of supply and of social organization to cope with the problems of a highly industrialized system. These are problems which the people and politicians have difficulty in defining—but they are all the more vexatious because they are so complex and obscure.

How Business Reacts

Business leaders are as aware as any other group in society of the climate of disorder and distrust that pervades these times. But most businessmen differ radically in their diagnosis of the causes of these social ills, and feel that they themselves are accused unjustly of being responsible for them. On the contrary, most businessmen see themselves as possessing both the ability and the desire to solve problems, not aggravate them—to give people what they really want, to "deliver the goods."

Businessmen are commonly at a loss to understand why they have been cast in the role of villains. They search for villains of their own—the enemies, conscious or unconscious, of business and the profit system. Hard times and the political challenge cause many corporate executives to go back to their own ideological roots, and induce a business backlash toward social and economic reformers. Many businessmen react to their critics and presumed enemies with suspicion and sometimes anger, rooted in a fear that the social goals and social controls being thrust upon them will undermine the vitality of business, and, in destroying its effectiveness and efficiency, will inflict great harm on a hitherto free and prosperous society.

The existence of widespread public disappointment with the performance of business, and business's counterattack, can thus be seen as part of a broader social dynamic. Serious tension has developed between the public expectations of business and the ability or willingness of the business system to meet the terms required for public approval without unduly restricting its autonomy or—as many businessmen fear—threatening the survival of private enterprise.

What is striking about the contemporary mood of the nation's business leadership is how similar it is to the mood of other groups in one important respect: a belief that control over its future is in the hands of other forces, and a feeling of impotence. For business, as for other groups, frustration often turns to hostility toward others in the society. Intense feelings of alienation and social antipathy began in the black community, spread to the children of the middle class, moved into the white working class, and have even affected the military and the police in America. This mood has now reached the business community. It is a remarkable society in which so many groups, even the "establishment," feel that "someone else" is in charge, "someone else" is to blame for what has gone wrong. During the series of conferences of business leaders in which we were observers, at the invitation of The Conference Board, we were struck by the frequently expressed view of businessmen that others than themselves were responsible for the nation's political, economic and social troubles—and those others were most frequently seen to be politicians, bureaucrats, the news media, educators, organized labor, young people, incompetent or lazy people looking not for work but for welfare.

Businessmen, also like other groups, tend to react very defensively when charged by others with responsibility for the nation's troubles, or for the widespread loss of confidence in its institutions. Economic troubles are commonly held to result from a crypto-socialism or excessive government interference that is undermining the effective working of a free-enterprise system; environmental problems, they contend, are distorted by environmental extremists; business corruption is blown up out of all proportion to reality by the foes of business—and business wrongdoing is in any case no worse than, and probably much less than, that of other elements in the society. Not all businessmen, by any means, take this complacent or defensive posture; some are deeply concerned

about the viability of business's traditional economic-policy views, the values of the business community as a whole, and the recent disclosures of unethical or illegal business behavior. However, even these concerned businessmen have been hesitant to criticize publicly those companies whose behavior has hurt business as a whole. Walter A. Haas, Jr., chairman of Levi Strauss, told a meeting of The Conference Board on "business credibility" on January 15, 1976:

> Unfortunately the public has seen heads of important major corporations involved in activities that are highly questionable and there has not been criticism from business. Punishment has generally been very gentle—until yesterday at least [referring to the action of the Gulf Oil board in dismissing its chairman and two top executives]. I guess it would be a very painful process but I do think it's time that business stopped drawing covered wagons in an ever-smaller circle and business people were critical of actions that have tarnished us all.

When asked how the business community itself might go about punishing a corporate malefactor, Mr. Haas replied:

> One suggestion has been for businessmen to set up a watchdog group to establish a code of ethical conduct—an association dedicated to finding and maintaining the highest standards of the profession. I just don't know if that's practical. Aside from that, I guess it would take a few courageous individuals who would be willing to speak up. I feel that some may be forthcoming.

Yet Mr. Haas, like so many businessmen at the conferences we attended, concluded that the problems of dubious morality and loss of confidence were not peculiar to the business community but affected the society as a whole:

> To me, this concern about business credibility is only a part of a much wider concern I have about general morality today. It occurs at all levels . . . a lack of concern for other people, an attempt to get away with all that you think you can get away with. I see this in every facet of society. . . . That the doubt about business credibility is part of a whole malaise of society disturbs me very much.

American Introspection

Rather then simply "throw off" on others, however, American businessmen do periodically meet to look intensively at *themselves,* their faults, their virtues, their values and responsibilities, and how they might make everything better. There is something uniquely American—foreigners might say "naively" American—about this belief of corporate leaders that they can improve business and the society as a whole by taking thought and counseling together.

Such hopeful attitudes are paralleled in America by those of business's critics, who have for many decades taken a reformist or "moral" line, rather than one calling for radical change in the capitalist system. By contrast, foreign critics of capitalism often eschew direct, ameliorist criticism of business behavior because they do not think it will make any difference. Inheriting a tradition of class struggle, the opponents of the corporations in Europe are more likely to see the problem of making corporations responsible to the broad society as one that necessitates radical change in the political-economic system. Ironically, the lack of this radical criticism of the system in the United States helps to explain the American business community's worry about its "image"—and its fear that a more radical attack will develop if its image continues to be tarnished.

Yet the very values that keep critics of American business from formulating an ideology that explicitly challenges capitalism—a pragmatic philosophy that respects what "works," an upward-striving ambition for limited goals (especially a higher standard of living), a privatism that regards politics as a game or a racket, or in any case a matter of limited importance, and a resentment toward government control—are shared by the business leadership itself.[1] Neither business nor its critics are able to stand sufficiently apart from the American orthodoxy to appreciate the relatively narrow parameters of their disagreement. As American labor and American intellectuals generally forgo radical attack on the system, American businessmen are resistant to the temptations of fascism that their European counterparts have in the past fallen victim to. Although American businessmen, as noted in the chapters that follow, have traditionally regarded themselves as the nation's dominant elite, their strong anti-government bias and their commitment to an ideology of "freedom" has made them immune to totalitarianism on the right, and even to the more moderate forms of "planning" accepted readily by businessmen in France, Scandinavia, Japan and elsewhere.

While few American businessmen are likely to be reassured by public criticism, the frequent attacks on the "morals," performance and influence of their firms are, in a sense, evidence of the stability of American capitalism and its broad public acceptance; periodic public vilification is the price American business pays for the absence of a serious socialist challenge. Yet such attacks can lead to legislative or regulatory actions that hamper business's freedom—and may reduce its profitability.

Anxiety About the System

There is another factor that helps to explain the outbreaks of tension between the corporations and the rest of the American society: the notion of American "uniqueness." The belief that there is something special about the United States has been a central theme in the consciousness of Americans since the earliest settlements; while Europe was the "old country," and was always "there," American society and civilization were the object of conscious creation. Americans felt that they were building a society that would be the cynosure of all mankind. John Winthrop said of the settlement at Massachusetts Bay, "We must consider that we shall be as a city upon a hill, the eyes of all people are upon us." The business executive who suggested, at one of the conferences, that "America is capitalism's last chance," was unconsciously echoing the belief that lay behind the Puritan migration to the new world—that "America is God's last chance."

The other side of this sense of American uniqueness is a feeling of pervasive insecurity. This unique experiment may fail. The dangers facing "the American free enterprise system"—somehow a system different even from that of other capitalist countries—runs as a motif throughout the history of American business opinion. This concern about the fragility of the American experiment (a counterstroke to the energy and optimism that are so much a part of the American ethos) runs from the *Federalist Papers* through the latest speeches made at a business conference.

Anxiety about the fragility of the American system—and the survival of free enterprise and democracy—are very much on the minds of U.S. business leaders these days. To what extent, they are asking, have the principles that have governed the relationship between business corporations and the rest of society become incompatible with rates of profit necessary to insure the continued existence and growth of capitalism in America? They perceive an inherent conflict between a largely independent corporate sector able to pursue its own economic objectives on one side, and, on the other, a popularly elected government dominated by the vast number of voters who seek to realize their own aims, whether these cripple business or not.

Businessmen have grown increasingly troubled about the apparent conflict between popular democracy and the traditional prerogatives of free enterprise. Is the conflict real and deep? Has corporate autonomy been rendered obsolete and even dangerous by the economic imperatives of a highly complex and highly integrated industrial society? Must the traditional atomistic enterprise system give way to a more closely coordinated and planned system—whether under the dominance of the great corporations, other social groups, or the government bureaucracy itself? Such profound ideological questions are very much on the American political agenda today.

The Importance of Ideology

This is not the first time in American history that such fundamental questions have been raised as a result of public discontent and hostility toward business, especially big business. Each of the last two earlier waves—the Progressive Era, 1902–1912, and the Great Depression, 1929–1939—resulted in significant changes in our political and economic system. What outcome will result from this third wave? That will depend not simply on technological imperatives but on political and social values and beliefs—that is, on ideologies, including the ideology of business.

The term "ideology" is often given a negative connotation; thus we say, "My opponents are ideologues, but I am interested in the truth." Yet when understood in its broadest sense, ideology can be seen as a cultural system, a way of organizing a particular, coherent view of society. Ideology functions not simply to advance a particular interest (a misconceived or anachronistic ideology may in fact be in conflict with the interests of those espousing it) but to enable people to orient themselves to a complicated and confusing world. In the words of the cultural anthropologist Clifford Geertz:

> Ideologies play a role in defining (or obscuring) social categories, stabilizing (or upsetting) social expectations, maintaining (or undermining) social norms, strengthening (or weakening) social consensus, relieving (or strengthening) social tensions.[2]

Ideology provides the concepts, the images, and, in crude form, the slogans and shibboleths of politics. But an ideology is most powerful when its tenets are regarded not only as means of manipulating others but of *understanding* complex reality. From this perspective, ideology is a critical aspect of communication, since it provides a means by which people can understand themselves, their concerns and problems, and give a sense of direction to their lives.

Many students of business argue that studying the ideology of business executives is likely to be uninformative. Businessmen, after all, are fundamentally men of action, not philosophers; what they think is less interesting and important than what they do. Yet this perspective seems shortsighted: one cannot so easily distinguish between attitudes and behavior. Attitudes and beliefs certainly shape human behavior, and are therefore as important to understand in the case of businessmen as of political leaders, labor leaders, intellectuals or any other influential group.

The ideas and ideals of businessmen are certainly important to the executives themselves. Businessmen, like any occupational or social group, are very concerned about understanding their role in society. Like all individuals, they want to have a clear sense of what their particular function is and how it fits into the overall goals and needs of the social system of which they are a part. They want to believe that what they are doing with their lives is appropriate and useful.

Some students of political change have argued that a critical factor that determines when a dominant social group begins to lose power is when it loses faith in itself. But for businessmen, who live "in the market" and whose products are particularly subject to the appraisal of others, faith in oneself seems to depend to an extraordinary degree on the regard of others. Hence, the importance of "public relations" to businessmen—not just as a means of selling products but of gaining respect for oneself. Since 1901, when John D. Rockefeller hired Ivy Lee to reshape his public image, executives of American business have been particularly conscious— some might say obsessed—with formulating a coherent justification of their role in American society that is convincing to their less affluent fellow citizens and enhances their self-regard.

Why Public Attitudes Matter to Business

A favorable public view of businessmen has not only personal value but economic and political importance as well. For, in a modern society, legitimacy is a critical dimension of political and economic stability. While the importance of public opinion is frequently exaggerated, there can be no question that the degree of congruence between the self-image and public image of business enhances the political strength and legitimacy of business. Conversely, this is why businessmen grow so anxious and apprehensive when they feel that they are held in low regard by the rest of the nation. There have always been cycles in public approbation and disapprobation of business in America, and the downswings can come with sudden and alarming speed. As Daniel Yankelovich has observed:

> Business is being criticized and called a bum today for doing the same things that made it a hero just a few years ago.

Business hasn't changed; society has changed. The period from the end of World War II to the late nineteen-sixties was a time when what people wanted and what business provided were perfectly synchronized. What has happened since then is that the values of the country have shifted. . . . About a decade ago, the public's expectations about business were so high that openness would inevitably have led to disappointment: The hero would sometimes have clay feet, and the people would be surprised by actual performance as against what they thought was happening. Now we've gone to the opposite extreme. People are so cynical, so paranoid, so mistrustful that openness has to help rather than hurt.

The business community's concern with the public's faith in it, though often excessive, contains an important insight: A society cannot function well without public confidence in its institutions and its leaders, and in the United States large business corporations and their executives are critical elements in a healthy and stable social order. It makes a big difference whether the institutions that dominate a society exercise their authority according to legitimate claims or whether the public regards their role as improper or illegitimate. The business community has every reason to be concerned about the American public's present lack of confidence in it. And the challenge now facing America's business executives is not to explain themselves better but to demonstrate that they take the public's concerns and criticisms seriously.

There is reason for concern that, if slower growth in physical output and real income should lie ahead for decades to come, as some economists believe, American business, even with the best of intentions, may be unable to accumulate the wealth and physical assets it wants in a way that is consistent with what the broad public wants—and intends to get through the political process. And, paradoxically, the dependence of business on the political process—and government aid—may continue to increase as executives find various reforms increasingly threatening to their business organizations as a result of slower growth of the economy as a whole. Intensified foreign competition, and the growing hazards of doing business abroad in a world with diminishing respect for the power and rights of multinational corporations, may also make U.S. business more dependent on government—and hence on the favor of voters generally. Like it or not, the political process will hold life-or-death power over the business corporations.

Looking for Love

In seeking public favor and political approval, American businessmen frequently act surprised that they are not loved —the good father who works hard but is not appreciated by his ungrateful and ignorant children. But some businessmen recognize that, with all their wealth and power, it is inevitable that they should be the object of more enmity or envy than affection. As one executive put it during the conferences in which we participated:

> If we are looking for passion and pity—forget it. We must stop berating ourselves and seeking pity. We can get respect but never be loved.

Yet it seems particularly hard for businessmen to recognize the legitimacy of other groups in the society—politicians, writers, academics, artists, and so on. The businessmen tend to see society in narrowly economic terms, and they see those persons who do not contribute directly to the productive process as parasitic or (to use the term of the physiocrats of the eighteenth century) "sterile." Their own high income and status perhaps inevitably tend to make them look down on others—and frequently to undervalue the contribution of others to the society and even to the productive process itself. The great advances in knowledge that have made possible a high industrial (or postindustrial) civilization have largely come from outside the business organizations themselves.

The social and political narrowness of America's business leaders, which the best-informed businessmen themselves recognize and lament, comes as a surprise in a nation that has called itself a "business civilization"—a nation in which, by and large, business has been held in high regard, and one that has had a remarkably stable political history unmatched by any other nation. At first glance, America's political stability, appetite for innovation, and indifference to radical social and economic change might seem uniquely congenial to developing an unusually thoughtful business leadership. In fact, the remarkable stability and homogeneity of the American political tradition has left its businessmen relatively indifferent to social and political questions. As our study will show, businessmen often betray a remarkable lack of sophistication about their social and political beliefs; this may be possible only in a society in which the position of business has been free from serious ideological challenge for virtually its entire history. The lack of sophistication American executives demonstrate in trying to reexamine their role and rethink their designs for the American society is matched only by their critics' lack of sophistication about business institu- tions, how they operate and why they work as well as they do.

Alternative Apocalypses

With social, economic, and technological strains intensi- fying, apocalyptical modes of thought are coming to dominate political rhetoric in the United States. Scientists assure us that continued economic growth will mean the end of human life on this planet, perhaps of all life, while representatives of our business leadership perceive additional government regula- tion or direction as signifying the end of capitalism, freedom, and civilization as we have known it. The apocalyptical rhet- oric, for all its negativism, sounds remarkably self-indulgent. It caters to our vanity by assuring us that there is something particularly important about the events that take place within our lifetime.

Such rhetoric is counterproductive; it arrests necessary change and adaptation of the American system. For business leaders, the margin for self-deception has become reduced; the political and social ideology through which business per- ceives the world has grown uncomfortably incongruent with the political and social environment in which business finds itself.

The well-being of the citizens of the United States will depend significantly on the degree to which the nation's busi- ness leadership is willing to adjust and reexamine its goals and structures. The future of the republic will in large measure be debated and decided in terms of the power and purposes of the corporation. This future will not, of course, rest exclusively in the hands of corporate executives—indeed, if it did, there would be little political urgency for business in this study. Much of it will depend on the political and ideological effectiveness of non- and anti-business forces in the society. Yet, as long as the privately owned corporation remains the central institutional mechanism for the production and distribution of goods and services, the views of businessmen on social and political issues will have a substantial impact on public policy. Their vision is important both because they are powerful and because their power will rest increasingly on the comprehensiveness and compassion of their vision.

The Conferences

Between September 1974 and September 1975 The Conference Board held a series of eight three-day meetings among top corporate executives to explore the current and future social and political role of business. Each conference was attended by between 35 and 55 business people, almost all of them the chief executive officers of American-owned and headquartered corporations. The private discussions among these business leaders are the source of the quotations and attitudes reported in this study.

There is a measure of unfairness in comparing the direct quotations of what businessmen said *ad lib* at the conferences with the well-thought-out and published views of their critics. This disparity was unavoidable, given the way this book was researched. We could hear what the business executives had to say, thinking out loud, but we had to depend on the written work of the scholars. Although the words of the businessmen may be rougher than those of the scholars, we think they are no less revealing of their true beliefs and attitudes.

The authors, who were ensured complete editorial independence by The Conference Board, have gone beyond a simple report on what businessmen said at these closed meetings to an analysis of their beliefs, their values, and their concerns. We have sought to achieve an analysis that goes beyond the words expressed.

The conferences provided an unusually rich opportunity to explore the views and attitudes of executives and to observe the personal interactions among executives as they examined issues which they felt were vital to their identity and institutional survival. Unlike most conferences, there was no distinction between audience and participants. The round-table format encouraged extensive and equal participation.

While some executives clearly felt more comfortable than others about participating in this collective effort, nearly all spoke out more freely than business executives customarily do in public nowadays.

In their roles as both businessmen and citizens, corporate executives generally feel frustrated about their inability to communicate effectively with the public. It is our hope that by presenting business views articulated in a forum *not* explicitly designated for public consumption, we have been able to cut through some of the public-relations aura that frequently characterizes business pronouncements. We hope this report will contribute to a better-informed public debate about the role of the corporation in America's future.

Each of the participants in the conferences was assured

anonymity, and thus virtually all the statements that appear in the book are unattributed. The authors' role at the conferences was largely confined to that of observers; we do not think our attendance inhibited the free and natural flow of discussion, although the reader must judge for himself the candor of the views expressed.

The sessions were not tape-recorded, and our report of the actual remarks made at the conferences derives from two sources: our own notes and the kindness of a number of executives in offering us copies of the notes they prepared for their own remarks.

Our agreement with The Conference Board specified that the identity of conference participants would remain confidential. All quotations below, unless otherwise identified, came from remarks made at the eight conferences in 1974–75. The businessmen who participated in the conferences were chairmen, presidents or high officers of their companies. The companies spanned the entire industrial spectrum. Many of them have substantial international operations, and some are among the nation's leading multinational corporations. Among those firms with 40 percent or more of their sales outside the United States are Ampex, Avery Products, Consolidated-Bathurst, Hughes Tool, IBM, Texaco, Exxon, BASF Wyandotte, and Bechtel. Many others represented in the seminars have 25 percent to 40 percent of their business overseas, including American Cyanamid, Beckman Instruments, Celanese, Cummins Engine, Del Monte Corporation, Dresser, Fluor Corporation, B. F. Goodrich, Oak Industries, Phillips Petroleum, and Textron. In all, more than 250 companies were represented; the 57 whose participants' ideas are incorporated in the text are listed in the Acknowledgments.

Our aim has been to present what we hope is an accurate and fair portrait of the thinking of America's business leaders during a particularly critical period in the development of American capitalism.

We are grateful to The Conference Board and particularly to Alexander B. Trowbridge, who was its president at the time this project was launched, for inviting us to undertake this study, on the occasion of the nation's Bicentennial. We should like to stress that the responsibility for the accuracy of this report and its interpretation of the thinking of the business community today are entirely our own.

L.S.

D.V.

CHAPTER TWO

Distrust of Government and the Political Process

THE ANXIETY OF corporate executives about the lack of public understanding and appreciation of their role in society is closely linked to their concern about their relationship with the government. Public policy, in their view, is formed in an adversary relationship—who wins is "up to the public."

"We must be perceived by the public as a social utility," said one executive. But many business leaders fear that the democratic political process is increasingly resulting in anti-business outcomes, whether by design or as a result of public ignorance or indifference to business needs for managerial autonomy and profit.

The executives at these conferences seemed unanimous in believing that government policy essentially reflects the immediate preferences of the majority of citizens; since, as they saw it, the preservation of the free enterprise system is becoming steadily less important to the public, government policy could be expected to encroach steadily upon the privileges and prerogatives of the management of privately owned institutions. The very fact that a growing number of issues before the Government concern proposals that many executives oppose is itself a sign of the weakening of public support for business; if corporations were better understood, their management of economic accumulations would not be subject to such political debate.

> *We must take the energy crisis out of politics.*

While the critics of business worry about the atrophy of American democracy, the concern in the nation's boardrooms is precisely the opposite. For an executive, democracy in America is working all too well—*that is the problem*.

During the latter half of the nineteenth century and the first half of the twentieth century, business relations with labor unions was the main concern of American executives, who saw unionism as a threat to managerial autonomy and corporate profits. The 1974–75 conferences suggest a sharp departure in executive thinking: anti-union outbursts (such as, "Letting the Wagner Act pass was the biggest mistake we ever made—it is at the root of all our troubles") were infrequent. On the contrary, unions were the nonbusiness institution that executives praised more than condemned.

> *Meany is a big opponent of socialism. American labor is the most conservative in the world. They don't care about participation in management.*

It is not the unions but government—and the popular pressures on government—that the business community sees as the central source of challenge to the viability and profit-

ability of corporate enterprise. Union demands have by no
means ceased to be a problem, but their challenge to corporate autonomy and profits is perceived as being most
dangerous when focused on the political process, not at the
bargaining table. It is when the unions clash with business
over public-policy issues that they become threatening.

George Meany outbeats us and outsmarts us every time.

Given a view of the political process in which the public's
opinions, as expressed through polls, are promptly moved
onto the political agenda and often become government
policy, executives conclude that their own ability to influence governmental decisions is being rapidly diminished.
Businessmen at these conferences felt, as one put it, that
"the power of wealth in politics is in a decline." It is not
clear to them when this trend began; some see the New Deal
as the turning point. Some would date the weakening of the
political influence of business at the federal level from the
early sixties, with President Kennedy's fight with the steel
industry and the subsequent rollback of steel price increases.
Coming after the Nixon Administration and in the midst of
the Ford Administration—both of which are generally regarded as very "pro-business"—the conferences were remarkable for the frequent assertions of belief that the relations
between business and government are the poorest in at least
a generation and are continuing to deteriorate.

*The businessman has a lower credibility in Washington
than that of any other group. The average businessman is
unconcerned about this problem. We are fighting for our
lives.*

I am asked to talk about the state of business-government relations. How could they get worse?

We are fighting a delaying action.

We are on the defensive, on the witness stand, forced to justify ourselves. It creates a division between business and government.

These businessmen perceive themselves as becoming more and more politically impotent. They see the inability of government policy makers to understand business as an ominous development: they are afraid that an expanded role for government would mean delivering their fates over to those who are either hostile or indifferent to their interests.

While there are some businessmen whose distrust of and bitterness toward the authority of the state are complete and unequivocal, the overwhelming majority believe that government does have a legitimate role to play in the society. Most executives support, in principle, the necessity for federal standards of environmental quality and believe that the community, acting through the government, has a responsibility to care for its less fortunate members.

Representatives of particular industries on occasion expressed their satisfaction with the performance of the government agencies entrusted with supervising or regulating particular areas of the economy. Generally speaking, however, government regulation of industry was roundly damned.

Many businessmen expressed their awareness and appreciation of the international responsibilities of the U.S. government and expressed their willingness to cooperate with the direction of its foreign policy in such areas as energy policy, food policy, and East-West trade, if only these would be clearly stated and competently managed. And some executives, as we shall see, can envision a substantial expansion of the scope of government intervention in the economy as necessary and perhaps inevitable.

Hostility Toward Government

Nonetheless, the dominant attitude of corporate executives toward governmental officials, whether elected or appointed, is one of hostility, distrust, and not infrequently, contempt. The following statements capture some of this sentiment:

> *Businessmen think that most elected officials would be somewhere else if they had the ability to do some better job.*

> *The government is full of bright, long-haired, arrogant young lawyers right out of Harvard Law School whose main goal in life is to harass us.*

> *We do our job, and the government messes things up.*

Much of this hostility is directed at "bureaucrats." Businessmen share a deep skepticism about the ability of government to do anything efficiently, and they believe that whenever possible the achievement of society's objectives is better left in their own hands. The reason for governmental inefficiency, businessmen invariably insist, is that public decisions are made without the discipline of the marketplace.

With the downfall of President Nixon as a result of Watergate, and the election of many liberals to the 1974 Congress,

the main concern of businessmen at the time of these conferences was directed at the elected politicians rather than
at the bureaucrats. The business executives were worried
about the shift in power from the executive to the legislative
branch; beyond their feeling of betrayal by Mr. Nixon and
their complaints about the lack of strong leadership coming
from President Ford, the businessmen had little complaint
about the Presidency; they appeared to regard it as their
chief hope for restraining and controlling government interference.

It is Congress that bears the brunt of their bitterness. Congress is seen as particularly vulnerable to the pressures of
those who lack appreciation of the contribution of business
to the nation and its economic well-being.

> *Congress is like the wife and mother with many children.*
> *If she gives more things to the children than her husband*
> *can afford, there has to be a period of belt-tightening until*
> *debts are paid off. There is only one place goods are going*
> *to come from for Congress to give away, and that is from*
> *people in industry and agriculture. So, when Congress gives*
> *goods away faster than people can produce, inflation results*
> *and some goods are taken away from everyone.*

> *Congress doesn't consider what we can afford when it votes*
> *social benefits.*

One senses that few words conjure up more negative con-
notations in the corporate lexicon than "politician." In the
eyes of the businessman, the politician is everything he himself is not; he is a glad-hander, a compromiser. He sells

himself to a wide diversity of people; he gives them what they want—or pretends to. Ironically, the business image of the politician corresponds closely to the liberal's stereotype of the business salesman, promoter, or Madison Avenue advertising executive—interested only in his own welfare, concerned only with the short run, manipulating people and public opinion for his own ends, essentially amoral. The businessman charges the politician, as the liberal charges the businessman, with narrow-minded pursuit of self-interest and with exerting a corrupting effect not only on his own institution but on the society as a whole.

> *It is up to each of us, not to some prostitute of a Congressman pandering to get reelected, to decide what should be done.*

> *Congress is filled with shortsighted, opportunistic thinkers who don't know economics or history.*

> *Congressmen are lawyers who couldn't succeed.*

> *If you have anyone who knows something in government, he is disqualified, so you get people who know nothing.*

The politician is seen as a sort of "confidence man." For the sake of election or reelection, he plays upon and manipulates the preferences of his constituents.

Businessmen feel that the typical politician, instead of tempering the distorted view of business the public gets from the educational system and the news media, magnifies it so that the public's hostility toward business is reinforced and aggravated.

The Irresponsible Electorate

Implicit in the distrust of politicians felt by many executives is a less than flattering view of the electorate. There is a striking contrast between business's view of the relationship between the citizen and his government and the relationship between the consumer or worker and his employer. Where many businessmen see the citizen-government relationship as manipulative and irresponsible on the side of the politicians and ignorant on the side of the voters, they commonly perceive the relationship of the firm to its constituencies, stockholders, employees, and particularly consumers, as epitomizing the ideals of responsibility and accountability.

In the marketplace, every person gets a vote every day. The market is more democratic than the government.

Executives are eloquent in their praise of consumer sovereignty. It is fair, it is efficient. A business, unlike a government program, can survive only if it succeeds in continually meeting the public's approval and needs, as manifest by their daily dollar votes of confidence in the marketplace.

The individual in the role of consumer is regarded as inherently responsible precisely because he or she is disciplined by the imperatives of economics. The consumer has finite financial resources and must weigh carefully the merits of every spending decision. If a wrong choice is made, the consumer suffers the penalties.

But business is, in turn, subject to the discipline of consumers, who can punish one producer and reward another on a moment's notice. The stakes for both business and consumers are real and immediate, and this encourages mutual responsibility and accountability.

By contrast, while the citizen-politician relationship also has serious economic consequences, businessmen see the electoral process as inherently irresponsible because it lacks immediate economic consequences, except, of course, where vote buying or the bribing of politicians is involved—acts which businessmen regard as perversions of the political process that result from the power with which government officials and politicians have been invested as the economic role of the state has grown.

Unlike the consumer, the voter is seen as having little incentive to exercise any economic constraint in asking for programs of direct benefit to himself. Why should he not vote for the politician who promises to appropriate increased funds for programs that will benefit him, provided that he does not expect his own taxes to rise proportionately—or more?

Alternatively, the businessman asks, Why shouldn't the politician, whose primary concern is to get elected, compete with the opposition in the extravagance of his promises? Moreover, once the politician has succeeded in getting elected, a similar dynamic is at work; he seeks greater expenditures of resources, especially for his own district, if the costs to his constituents seem trivial—or at least uncertain—compared to the direct benefits. To be sure, raising taxes to pay for programs is a constraint that voters and politicians take seriously when perceived costs outweigh anticipated benefits. The ideology of business asserts that, in general, the costs of government programs do outweigh their benefits, and it is the aim of business conservatives to convince the electorate and a majority of politicians of the correctness of that proposition.

But business executives blame themselves for having been politically inept and for not getting deeply enough involved in the political process.

The Dangers to Business

What are the likely consequences of the lack of adequate participation of business in politics according to business executives? They see one danger as paramount—that government decisions, however well intentioned, will undermine the independence of the business corporation. They see mistaken government policies resulting from ignorance of business and the factors necessary to the successful performance of the economic system. They express alarm about the "economic illiteracy" of government officials, politicians, and the general public (though, somewhat paradoxically, expressing considerable skepticism about the competence—or at least the judgment—of economists themselves, especially liberal economists). Businessmen, they feel, must strive to correct the economic illiteracy of politicians and government officials.

> *If Congress passes legislation without considering the input of business, we will have over-regulation, socialization and the nationalization of enterprise, as in Europe.*

> *Too many government officials do not understand the critical role of corporate profits in contributing to the amelioration of economic injustice.*

> *Congress has no appreciation of the process of capital formation.*

> *Government agencies don't understand business.*

Corporate executives are particularly concerned these days about the additional regulation of private economic activity in such areas as consumer and environmental protection and occupational health and safety. They see new pension regulations as seriously weakening the independence of the private sector. One executive put it graphically:

> *My industry is regulated up to its neck. You are regulated up to your knees. And the tide is coming in.*

Not only are the regulations costly, say the businessmen, but they complicate and confuse the process of corporate decision-making and have heavy hidden as well as direct costs. They threaten the functioning of a "free" economy and its ability to innovate and respond rapidly and creatively to economic opportunities. Businessmen assert that government regulations made now with the best of intentions will severely limit their future choices; future business earnings will have already been preempted and committed by public policies.

The government agencies which today bear the brunt of the executives' ire are the new ones whose insulation from business influence makes their decisions unpredictable and, as they see it, hazardous to the ability of business to make adequate profits. It seems that almost every executive has some bureaucratic horror story to relate of his experience with some allegedly unreasonable official from the Consumer Product Safety Commission, the Occupational Safety and

Health Administration, or the Environmental Protection Administration. The Congressional decision to reverse automobile seat-belt requirements, in response to widespread consumer complaints, was triumphantly cited several times during different conference sessions as a typical example of the lack of foresight in many well-intentioned government actions.

While few executives would abolish these agencies, many feel that their regulations have become obsessive and are made with no understanding of their economic costs.

> *The harassment of the businessman by the government bureaucracy hampers productivity. I spend a large part of each day with a lawyer or two, protecting myself from possible prosecution.*
>
> *I spend too much time each day complying with government regulations.*
>
> *The social responsibility of business should be decided by the boards of directors. But now it is decided by Congress. We're having a major intrusion of government into formerly private decisions.*
>
> *EPA is an absolute necessity. Yet as we are making progress, it is growing.*

While the new regulations seem especially annoying to executives, those in the long-regulated industries such as the railroads and public utilities have plenty of their own complaints.

> *We have been regulated for nearly one hundred years, and we have never gotten used to being told how to run our business.*

We have had price controls for fifty years, and we think it's terrible.

Capital Formation

Business executives regard the rise of government social welfare expenditures as inevitably inflationary and hold it responsible for weakening the ability of the economic system to generate the capital required for expansion. And they contend that, as government outlays rise, the tax system discourages saving and undermines the investment on which the capitalist system depends for its vitality.

The issue of inadequate capital formation was much on the minds of the businessmen attending the 1974–75 conferences. In the summer of 1975 the Ford Administration, in response to the pressures of business groups and the securities industry, launched a campaign for new tax incentives to encourage saving and investment, arguing that they were essential if the United States were to overcome a looming capital shortage and to achieve faster growth in productivity, total output, and employment. Businessmen favoring additional tax incentives for investment maintained that a prosperous and stable economy would tend to benefit all groups in the society.

Undoubtedly the nation faces huge capital demands to make possible growing investment in energy development, pollution abatement and environmental protection, mass transit, the processing of raw materials, and outlays on new plant and equipment. But the issue of just how much capital formation would be required, how to achieve it, and how to relate it to other social objectives is an extremely complex economic and political problem. Estimates by economists of investment requirements a decade ahead varied by hundreds of billions of dollars, with different assumptions on necessary or desirable rates of national economic growth. The redistribution of income implicit in a shift from favoring consumption to favoring investment was an issue certain to divide liberals from conservatives.

The problem was further complicated at the time of the 1974–75 meetings because, with the economy in its deepest slump since the Depression, there was no immediate capital shortage problem. Nor was it entirely clear that if and when the economy got back to full employment there would be such a problem. However, if a capital shortage were to be avoided in years to come, it seemed essential to avoid huge federal budget deficits that would constitute a drain on national savings when the economy returned to full employment. Some conservative, as well as liberal, economists warned that tax cuts, though intended to increase the flow of savings and investment, might actually be counterproductive if they went too far in reducing the Treasury's tax revenues and increasing its borrowing needs.

Nevertheless, most businessmen at these meetings were convinced that taxes on business and on investors were too high, and they were seeking tax relief. Since they recognized the difficulty of achieving substantial tax cuts at existing levels of government spending and feared the inflationary consequences of creating still larger budget deficits, they sought the solution in cuts in both taxes and government expenditures. President Ford followed this line in his 1975 proposal for matching cuts of $28 billion in taxes and $28 billion in expenditures. A similar trade-off had been demanded in 1968 at the expense of delaying a tax cut. Although the Revenue and Expenditure Control Act of 1968 did slow down spending, it did not do so for long because of the expenditures for Vietnam. It was, nevertheless, considered a moral victory by many fiscal conservatives because the debate preceding the legislation made large segments of the public conscious of the cost of "big government."

What Is Business's "Social Responsibility"?

The businessmen attending these conferences appeared to regard the term "social responsibility" as a pretentious, annoying and somewhat outmoded cliché, invented not by businessmen but by "sociologists." The earlier period in the 1950's and 1960's, when businessmen could decide for themselves how and how much their companies should become involved in social issues, appeared to them to be over; government was now telling business what its social responsibilities were, and businessmen didn't like it.

> *Social responsibility has become a burden on productive America. Our system cannot survive the pressures of the next ten years with our inability to make choices among alternatives.*

> *How can the productive sector carry the nonproductive?*

> *We must limit our expectation and recognize that while we can afford anything, we cannot afford everything.*

The central tension of American capitalism, according to the common business view, is between people's rising aspirations and the inability of the American economic system to satisfy them without weakening its long-term viability. People's desires are rising faster than the productive capacity of the American economy.

We may be engulfed by a rising tide of entitlement.

Our enemies want cradle-to-grave security for everyone.

Desires are becoming social demands.

Transfer payments are a form of redistribution of wealth— the trend began in the New Deal and shows no signs of stopping.

There is a real sense of crisis among executives, a concern that "transfer payments"—money given by the government without services rendered by the recipients—are rising faster than total output, and the delicate balance between consumption and investment is being tilted in favor of consumption. What makes this trend particularly ominous to businessmen now is that it is occurring at a time when the long-term growth prospects of the economy look increasingly dim; when "the management of surplus is a thing of the past."

Businessmen see a vicious cycle: The public uses the franchise to vote itself more goods and services because it is displeased at the pace at which these are being delivered by the profit sector; these public outlays reduce the rate of private investment; and this results in a further reduction of the rate of private production. The goose that lays the golden eggs is, they fear, being strangled.

The threat to American living standards is heightened because, while people are demanding more and more from government, "we are moving from an economy of abundance based on cheap capital, cheap energy, cheap natural resources, into an economy of scarcity based on expensive capital, expensive energy, and expensive natural resources."

> *Americans are learning for the first time in the postwar period that a high standard of living is not guaranteed.*

> *We have had cheap energy, food, and money. We are facing a traumatic transition.*

The Central Issue: Role of the State

For executives, the central drama of contemporary American politics is the rapidly growing role of the state in attempting to supplement the economic wants of citizens that are unmet in the marketplace. This, in their view, represents the gravest threat to the survival of the free enterprise system. Many businessmen perceive a growing tension between the imperatives that govern private capital accumulation and the principles of a democratic polity. The two major responsibilities of the state in a democratic capitalist society— to maintain its legitimacy and to insure an environment conducive to capital accumulation—appear, from the perspective of business, to have come into conflict.

> *The balance has shifted from a generative to a distributive society.*

> *The normal end of the democratic process gives unequal people equal rights to pursue happiness in their own terms. There is a difference between a free enterprise system and a democracy which we also espouse.*

> *The have-nots are gaining steadily more political power to distribute the wealth downward. The masses have turned to a larger government.*

> *Each of these enlightened masses is demanding a larger share of the pie so the share left for the entrepreneur is smaller. Thus, the incentives are less for the guy who scrambles to the top of the heap.*

Not only does the public demand collective goods from government which, by definition, cannot be provided by the market, but the public is increasingly turning to the state to provide goods that were formerly allocated by the market-place. As the cost of various commodities increases, the public is unwilling to continue to let the market allocate them; it demands that they be distributed by criteria other than that of the ability to pay. Many businessmen are willing to accept in principle that it is unfair to demand that the poor suffer disproportionately as a result of the sharp increases in the prices of food and energy, and that some modification of the market mechanism is called for in the interests of social justice. But their concern is that more and more commodities are being considered necessities rather than luxuries:

> *No one, after all, complains about the scarcity of caviar; we accept the fact that our limited supplies of this commodity will be distributed according to the marketplace. But we*

feel differently about bread or milk. More and more goods and services are being classified like bread rather than caviar.

The public is demanding more and more goods. If they can't get them through the marketplace, they will get them through government.

How do we allocate scarcity in a private enterprise system? We are great at allocating surplus, but can we allocate scarcity via private enterprise?

The government's response to rising expectations is to control prices and allocate rather than improve supplies.

Who is responsible for this "rising tide of entitlement"? Business by and large blames itself; the problem is defined as a classical illustration of the perils of success:

We have been hoist with our own petard. We have raised expectations that we can't deliver on.

We have promised too much in our enthusiasm.

We have gotten carried away.

We have to get away from an economy of endless consumption.

We have created our own Frankenstein's monster.

The public has been persuaded all too well by relentless advertising that the quality of one's life is most appropriately defined by the amount of one's material possessions. The American public has been convinced of the importance of not only a chicken in every pot, but also of a detached single-family dwelling, two cars in the garage, a cabin in a pleasant, remote, wooded area, meat each night, and a boat. To these private possessions Americans have recently added a variety of social goals: high, continuous employment, adequate medical care, day-care facilities, unlimited educational opportunity, an adequate income for retirement—"cradle-to-grave security." Not only does the American public increasingly expect these things, but it expects them immediately.

The Commitment to Growth

The new problem may be to reduce the public's expectations of an ever-rising standard of living and ever greater security. Some executives are intrigued these days by the anti-materialism of the young, as they worry that "we may not have the resources to continue the exponential growth curve."

> *We should take the message of the young more seriously. Maybe the quality of life is not identical with the quantity of goods.*
>
> *There is a relationship between the resource scarcity and the values of the young.*

However, by and large, the business community remains hostile to the idea of nongrowth. Executives believe that a maximum-growth society is not only most congruent with the achievement of the objectives of their own companies, but is absolutely essential as a means of forestalling pressures for redistribution of income.

Business's willingness to accept slower growth depends crucially on how it comes about. Will it take place through the restrictions placed on corporate investment by the environmentalists? If so, business will fight it. But if a declining growth rate is seen as a result of economic forces simply beyond the control of business, executives say they will do their best to convince others to accept the dictates of the market and get along with less. They still want the *potential* growth of the economy to be realized, and oppose a policy of slow growth or no growth.

Growth must be stable and result from balanced private saving and investment, not from bigger and bigger government spending, which will breed endless inflation and wreck the capitalist system.

> *Recession is like a sore. Inflation is like cancer.*
>
> *Inflation decimates our ability to form capital and thus produce wealth.*
>
> *High inflation rates are caused by high demand: competition for capital.*
>
> *Continuing high inflation at the current double-digit level will put enormous strains on our political and business structures. In the short range it will probably expand the government's role in financing; in the longer range, it may lead to socialism or some form of totalitarianism.*

If the corporate sector is unable to generate sufficient capital to meet its future requirements, it will have no choice but to rely upon government for financing. The financial weakness of the utilities, airlines, railroads is seen as proto-typical: it demonstrates the result of oppressive government regulation and the insensitivity of government policy planners to the imperatives of capital accumulation.

All regulated industries are in trouble.

And the businessmen fear that inflation and a continuing trend toward government financing, subsidy, and control will mean the weakening of all private industries.

I am worrying about the socialization of our investment decisions if inflation doesn't get under control.

We are moving from an incentive society to a controlled one.

The battle is being lost. More and more industries are wards of the state.

Industry will soon find itself put into a position where it is not able to produce, and government will take over by default.

At this rate we'll soon need a Medium Business Administration.

Many industries cannot survive another bout of 12 percent inflation rates.

With high inflation, the only source of capital is government.

The Defense of Hard Times

While many executives were obviously unhappy with the economic decline that was going on during the period of these conferences, they were far more concerned with the long-term economic viability of capitalism in the United States. Those who expressed themselves on this issue tended to see the recession's positive side:

> *This recession will bring about the healthy respect for economic values that the Depression did.*

> *People need to recognize that a job is the most important thing they can have. We should use this recession to get the public to better understand how our economic system works. Social goals are OK, provided the public is aware of their costs.*

> *It would be better if the recession were allowed to weaken more than it will, so that we would have a sense of sobriety.*

> *We need a sharp recession.*

Some businessmen hoped the slump would restore sanity to the public and a renewed respect for the role of business. When the economic system is performing well, people tend to take business for granted. As their expectations increase, they forget what things cost; they believe in the free lunch. The longest period of peacetime prosperity in American history was accompanied by a steady escalation of the government's social programs. As long as prosperity appeared likely to continue indefinitely, the public had little incentive to question the costs of these programs; they could all be paid for out of an expanding GNP.

The businessmen blamed themselves for doing little to weaken this euphoria, for going along with the notion that expanded government social-welfare programs, far from constituting a drain on the resources of the private sector, represented a source of future profits and growth. There were billions of dollars of government contracts available to corporations interested in committing their managerial skills not only to national defense, but to constructing mass transit facilities, waste-disposal systems, schools, hospitals, etc.

But the recession had put to rest talk of constructing a "social-industrial complex," and many executives expressed the hope that its impact would be much longer lasting. Hard times, somewhat paradoxically, drive business to the right— make it more hostile to government social programs, more determined in the face of the threat of economic breakdown and political hostility from the rest of the population to preserve its own prerogatives and autonomy.

Political Participation by Business

Executives hope to deal with the conflict they believe exists between the underlying values and goals of government and business by participating more actively in political policy making to make it "more responsible."

> *We need more business involvement in the policy process.*

> *If you don't know your senator on a first-name basis, you are not doing an adequate job for your shareholders.*

> *Chief executive officers must talk directly to government officials.*

> *Each of us should plan to spend one weekend a month in Washington.*

We should not have to rely on lobbyists to make our case.
Elected officials should already be responsible.

Businessmen are disturbed about the adversary system they feel has developed between business and government. Although aware that government officials and business executives do have different constituencies, they do not see that as presenting an insurmountable obstacle to improved communication between them. Remarkably, although much of the public, especially after the Nixon years, sees business and government as excessively close, even corruptly close, business executives generally perceive a wide and still widening gulf between business and government.

The concern of business is that government base its programs and regulations on sound economic criteria. Since executives define the differences between public and private officials as fundamentally one of misunderstanding and suspicion—government policy makers are simply unaware of the economic implications of their programs and see businessmen as having little credibility—they think better communications should lead to better-informed and more competent government policies.

Many executives see themselves as a group whose policy positions merit particular attention because, ultimately, it will be the resources from their institutions that bear the costs of government decisions.

We need more political sophistication. We have to tell a
state considering additional restrictions on business: "The
next plant doesn't go up here if that bill passes."

We must deflate false expectations planted by demagogues.

We should cease to be patsies and start to raise hell.

For God's sake, in the words of the next generation, "Get involved."

Many executives see the pattern of government policies over the last decades as a continual series of defeats for the business point of view. On one set of issues after another—environmental protection, consumer protection, occupational safety, pension reform, increased social-welfare appropriations—business has found itself on the defensive. The issues were first raised by the critics of business, and the proposed reforms were almost automatically opposed by business. The result was predictable: not only were innumerable programs that business opposed enacted, but the public's image of business as a negative, irresponsible, selfish force, insensitive to social needs and only concerned with its own interests, was confirmed. Some businessmen would like to reverse this negativism:

> *We are insufficiently sensitive to the social and political implications of what we do. We have tunnel vision. The government role in our lives is pervasive.*
>
> *We keep getting involved in policy areas after it is too late.*
>
> *We must get to problems before they get politically hot.*
>
> *We have to stop automatically opposing every program that we don't like.*

They contend that business interests would be better safe-guarded if business began to play a more active role in identifying, and then helping to resolve, policy issues *before* they become objects of political controversy. Business should try to structure political debates so that it is not invariably found on the side of the "opposition." It should plan an active, rather than simply a reactive, role in policy formation to enhance both its public image and political effectiveness.

> *We should be able to foresee social problems better than government and thus head them off.*

> *Business will have to reexamine its social impact to avoid getting into trouble. Unless we learn to swim, we will drown.*

Corporate executives see their performance at fault in another respect. In many cases, government intervention in the economy has, in fact, been at the insistence of corporations themselves.

> *We need to set a better example by not going to Washington for help.*

> *We have got to stop inviting government into areas where it doesn't belong.*

Executives want to be consistent in their behavior toward government. They do not want to be responsible for any unnecessary increase in government expenditures or government regulation.

But they feel politically weak and outnumbered. They recognize that in a democratic system they desperately need allies among the rest of the population. Many business leaders expressed interest in forming an alliance of the "productive" sector against the "nonproductive."

The unions are economic royalists too.

Meany is the best ally we have. Unions have knowledge of costs, margins, profits. We need an alliance between the capital sector and organized labor to protect the free enterprise system against anybody else.

It is unreasonable to expect labor to identify with us. We should just focus on specific areas of agreement.

Executives whose firms are currently unionized frequently expressed considerable respect for labor's political skills.

Recognizing the limits of the ability of union leadership publicly to identify with management, some businessmen nonetheless felt fairly encouraged about the possibility of labor-management alliances around specific issues, such as the excessive costs of product safety regulations, environment regulations, tariff protection, export subsidies or other help against foreign competition. Several executives argued that the firm's most important public was its employees:

The best and only forum we have is our companies. We have to have employees identify with the businesses. If the company does well, then they have the opportunity to do well.

The educational process starts at home.

Your first responsibility is to educate your own employees in the basic principles of economics.

We have been negligent in educating our own people to the important role of business in making our society work. . . . They don't seem to understand that their success is

directly linked to the success of management. They have
little or no appreciation of the fact that their jobs, their
prospects of an improved standard of living in the future,
their chance of advancement are all tied to the success of
the business enterprises in which they participate.

Workers constitute a special category of the electorate, and the physical presence on the corporation's premises enables management to communicate with them without the mediation of the press, television, and the educational system. But what of the rest of the public? Businessmen believe the loyalties of the public can go either way—toward business or against it. While business cannot count on much support beyond its own ranks (the number of top-level managers and owners of smaller enterprises is about 10 percent of the population), it commands at least as much popular support as its radical critics. The survival of the free enterprise system thus rests on the attitudes of some four-fifths of the public. They must somehow be persuaded that a major redistribution of wealth would not be in their own best interests:

We have to convince the have-nots that the way they can
become haves is not by tearing down our system but by
supporting us.

One executive commented that business should not be misled by the polls.

Deep down in their hearts, most people trust us more than
they do any other institution. We can still win their loyalty.

But the public, many businessmen feel, is wrecking the enterprise system out of ignorance.

The public really doesn't want to destroy the free enterprise system. They don't know what they are doing.

Every day in a piecemeal way, the public unwittingly destroys the free market.

Free enterprise, corporate executives contend nowadays, will not be destroyed by an apocalypse—they do not anticipate a socialist revolution—rather it will be inadvertently transformed and finally wiped out by a multitude of public policies, each appearing reasonable in its own terms. The very foundation of the system of private capitalist accumulation will be destroyed, in short, not so much out of malice—only one in ten genuinely wishes it ill—but out of ignorance and misunderstanding.

Criticism is a function of ignorance, not subversiveness.
People are destroying business who don't really want to.

According to American business leaders, the implications of the lack of recognition by the public of its close dependence on the economic achievements of business are ominous.

The American capitalist system is confronting its darkest hour.

At this rate business can soon expect support from the environmentalists. We can get them to put the corporation on the endangered species list.

There is a hole in the ship of free enterprise, and I see torpedoes ahead.

We should not be misled by the appearance of a light at the end of the tunnel. It is probably an oncoming train.

*What is the future of business-government relations? That
question makes an unwarranted assumption. It assumes
that we are going to continue to have business.*

"The British Are Coming"

Ironically, if any one slogan can be said to describe the
mood of executives at the Bicentennial of the founding of
our republic, it would be "The British Are Coming." The
precipitous decline of the British economy haunted each
conference; executives saw the decay of business enterprise
in Britain as a precursor of their own.

*If we don't take action now, we will see our own demise.
We will evolve into another social democracy like those
you see across the pond.*

The main threat to American business is no longer conceived to be communism. Since Mr. Nixon's opening of
closer relations with the Soviet Union and China, American
businessmen have rushed to set up trade deals with the communists. No, it is the threat of an inefficient and anti-business
socialism, as they conceive Britain's economy to be, that
alarms them.

*We are following England to disaster, trying to beat them
where they are going.*

We are heading to the basement to join Great Britain.

*England is our future over the next decade. First, they got
the dole, then we got our relief. First, they had socialized
medicine, then we got Medicaid and Medicare. First, they*

*had nationalized industry, now our utilities are in danger of
being taken over by the government. It is now 1975: after
199 years, isn't it about time we got free of England?*

We are like Britain in the 50's after Churchill's fall.

The importance of England to businessmen is not hard
to explain. It was the birthplace of industrial capitalism, and
it dominated the world economy in the nineteenth century,
as the United States has done through most of the twentieth.
England gave us the most important explanations and justi-
fications of the capitalist system and the sanctity of private
property, our legal system, much of our political philosophy,
the corporate form, and, not least significant, much of the
capital that made American industrialism itself possible.
England is the nation that Americans have traditionally
identified with most closely; we are bound to it by similar
economic and political systems, and by language and culture.
And a great many American businessmen have had direct
business involvement in Britain since World War II and
know its troubles at first hand.

American businessmen believe that the economic difficulty
in which England currently finds itself results from the actions
of British businessmen themselves, as well as from the
erosion of public support for the interests of British capital.
The American businessmen feel that their British counterparts have been more preoccupied with status than with being
really good managers. This was said to us by an English
businessman:

*We have failed; failed to listen to changes in our society
outside our business; failed to participate in the processes*

of our government; failed to build a constituency of support within our firms. We failed to communicate what we do, why we are in business, the need for participation in the political process.

A refrain heard at virtually every conference was that the British business community laid the basis for the reduction of its role by devoting insufficient energies to educating the British public about the linkage between a financially healthy business system and the welfare of the population as a whole. They "failed to educate" the public and allegedly withdrew from active participation in the political process, leaving the way open for the triumph of political forces opposed to their interests.

England made fairness more important than growth.

The British experience has given U.S. executives a growing sense of their own isolation—and importance. Many American businessmen see themselves as trustees of the principles and practices of capitalism, the defenders of what is left of the free enterprise system.

CHAPTER THREE

Why Most Businessmen Reject National Planning

DEEPLY CONCERNED about the contraction of their own political base—roughly coterminous with the Republican party—and about diminishing public support for the traditional free enterprise ideology, many businessmen have begun to fear that capitalism and democracy may be incompatible in the long run. There were frequent suggestions at the conferences of business executives that the American political system would have to be "reformed" to reduce the vulnerability of government to broad citizens' pressures:

> *Can we still afford one man, one vote? We are tumbling on the brink.*

> *We are terribly scared within this room. We are in serious trouble. We need to question the system itself: one man, one vote.*

> *One man, one vote has undermined the power of business in all capitalist countries since World War II. The loss of the rural vote weakens conservatives.*

75

A number of executives spoke vaguely of the need for "war-time discipline," and "a more controlled society."

What would these executives do if everyone's ability except their own to translate his preferences into government policy was seriously curtailed? The businessmen at these meetings did not address that question; they did not regard it as a real possibility. Their hopes for political-economic change were directed essentially toward a return to a more liberalistic social order, rather than movement toward a more collectivist state. Indeed, the businessmen appeared to sense that the security of their own corporations depends not on transforming the political system into one that they can dominate, but rather on preserving the existing legal and constitutional system; and that it is the basic legitimacy of the state that stands between the corporation and an increasingly hostile public.

They were thinking mainly in terms of drastic cuts in government expenditures, a revision of the tax laws to spur investment, more "rational" consumer-protection and environmental-protection legislation, and elimination of much other government regulation, restrictions on the political activity of unions, and an end to government budget deficits. And, since they believed so much in the worth of such policies, they did not dismiss the possibility of convincing a majority of the electorate of their merit and essentiality.

Corporate executives may feel harassed by the large number of nonbusiness groups making demands on business through the political process. But most recognize that this is preferable to these same groups *not* using the legal and political processes and the constitutional system to make demands on business because they believe the system is stacked and fixed against them, and instead resorting to direct, radical action. Except for an occasional eccentric, business leaders have not publicly and explicitly questioned any aspect of the nation's democratic institutions and procedures. While criticisms of the one man, one vote principle surfaced innumerable times at these conferences, no executive has raised this issue publicly. Executives, like all serious participants in the political process, are at least publicly bound by the norms of the political culture, and those norms presently include an unquestioned acceptance of the principle of democracy.

The Need for Reform

Nonetheless, some executives argue that "We can no longer muddle through," and wonder aloud whether our current constitutional system, conceived nearly two hundred years ago, is appropriate for the conditions of advanced capitalist production. A few insist that business corporations need to respond to increasingly strong and urgent social demands and pressures in a way that will maintain the incentive system.

> *We in business must recognize that all members of society have economic needs as basic as our own that must and will be satisfied by voluntary actions, by law, or by force in our future economic and social environment.*

> *The have-nots are tired of waiting. We will have to satisfy a variety of social demands in a system that will not be growing as rapidly. Can we keep our free enterprise*

system as well as our liberties? It is up to us: We have to
make sacrifices, share decision-making, get a smaller share
of the pie, yet still be responsible for economic performance
and productivity. Can we do this?

If business is to accomplish this feat, a minority of business leaders say, a major restructuring of the pattern of business-government relations is required.

Is any elected representative democracy capable of long-range planning? We don't have a democratic system designed for coping with the modern world.

Our government is simply not organized to make cost-benefit analyses.

In spite of all our wealth, we cannot solve all problems at the same time. We must establish priorities.

We will be forced to do a lot of things we don't want to do. The question is the wisdom of these policies.

It is on this issue—the nature of the needed restructuring —that much of the current debate within the business community focuses. Virtually all executives agree that government, as it currently functions, is ill-suited to meet the requirements of a modern, advanced capitalist economic system. The economic system has evolved significantly over the last two hundred years, while the nation's governmental mechanisms have grown archaic.

I think we are long overdue for a serious examination and major overhaul of our system of government. . . . Under

*conditions of today's technology, it takes at least eight to
ten years to work out our problems. We must tackle those
problems through officials whose vision stops at a horizon
only two to six years away at most, when we then again ask
them to account for their current performance.*[1]

The government responds to decisions on short-time bases
—the intervals between election years—while many problems
the nation confronts increasingly require a longer time horizon. Corporations themselves do plan on a longer time
horizon—five-, ten-, or even twenty-year plans are not un-
common in industry—but the increasing interdependence of
business and government means that the undisciplined democratic process is now more disruptive for business. Governmental policy introduces a critical element of unpredictability
and uncertainty into corporate decision-making. Vice President Rockefeller was quoted by the *San Francisco Examiner
& Chronicle* on June 12, 1975:

People in politics tend to think in two-year, four-year, or
six-year cycles, depending on the office they hold or serve.
But industry cannot operate in such a framework. Business
planning must run in different, usually longer, cycles, up to
ten years, even longer.

Businessmen are chagrined because federal policies affecting business are not only inconsistent over time but are also
inconsistent at any given time. The "managerial nightmare"
that passes for public administration in the United States,
they assert, could be tolerated as long as the overall rate of
capital accumulation and economic growth remained suffi-

ciently high. But as the long-term viability of the corporate sector becomes problematic, the price of legislative and administrative decentralization becomes excessive. It does not encourage business faith in the soundness of government decision-making to have agencies working at cross-purposes —say, for the Federal Energy Office to press for energy development while the policies of the Environmental Protection Agency work, in effect, to discourage it.

The myriad cross-purposes are a reflection, on the administrative level, of the conflicting priorities legislated by Congress, a process toward which businessmen, with their purposeful and often one-directional cast of mind, are unsympathetic and hostile. They see that the legislature makes all sorts of regulations and sets all sorts of goals, considering each decision on an *ad hoc* basis without understanding the broader picture.

The problem lies even deeper than that of conflicting priorities or competing policies. The government does' not know what it is doing; it lacks any but the most rudimentary mechanisms to determine the cost of programs. In such areas as environmental and consumer protection, the government acts ignorantly and impetuously, as the businessmen see it. They charge that the goals mandated by the Clean Air Act are economically unfeasible and that government policy on catalytic converters, phosphates and seat belts have been inconsistent and misguided.

Dissatisfied with the performance of government, most would simply have government do less, but a few business executives—in a sense, the "avant-garde"—would seek to have government perform more effectively and provide better support for a private sector that is strong and viable, and thus capable of assuring that the American economy remains domestically vital and internationally competitive for decades to come.

The Case for Planning

A small but growing number of business leaders believe that to meet crucial national problems the United States government should engage in some form of economic planning. For instance, Henry Ford II has said that the auto industry and others need to learn to live with dwindling supplies of oil and other materials, and hence there is a concomitant need for national planning in order to match scarce resources with consumption in an equitable and efficient manner. Mr. Ford has also suggested that the government should consider something like the Reconstruction Finance Corporation (launched by President Hoover and continued by President Roosevelt) "to make large amounts of capital available to industrial concerns and banks" that cannot raise money "because of the collapse of equity markets and shortages of loan funds." [2]

The term "national planning" has a wide variety of meanings, ranging from the provision of more information and long-range forecasts by government to programs involving detailed allocation of resources and investment under government guidance or control. Virtually all businessmen sympathetic to the planning idea are found at the mild and noninterventionist end of the spectrum; what they want is a system that would preserve capitalism, leave the control of the means of production largely in private hands, and keep capital accumulation and investment by corporations as the driving force of the economy—but with better coordination and long-range direction to meet national goals. Efforts by government to look farther ahead and to gather, analyze, and publish the information on which it is basing its own policy decisions would, according to business proponents of planning, help private industry to make its own planning decisions without governmental coercion of the private sector. Industries would still be free to make their own investment decisions, but they would do so on the basis of more complete information about long-term trends as affected by government policies. Not only the administration but Congress, private industry, labor, and other groups in the society would participate in the ongoing national debate over planning and in the establishment of national goals. Its proponents concede that planning may have its flaws and dangers, but maintain that the traditional planless approach has already proved its capacity for producing social and economic disasters.

Much of the current debate about planning in the United States focuses on the proposal of the Initiative Committee for National Economic Planning (a group headed by the Nobel Prize-winning economist Wassily Leontief and Leonard Woodcock, president of the United Auto Workers, but including a number of prominent businessmen such as Robert Roosa, partner in Brown Brothers Harriman Co.; Michael Blumenthal, chairman of Bendix; Irwin Miller, chairman of Cummins Engineering; and John R. Bunting, Jr., chairman of the First Pennsylvania Bank). This group maintains that:

> In a modern economy, planning is not a matter of preference or ideology. It is one of immediate need. In its absence we will all suffer. This suffering is avoidable. . . . We believe

that economic leadership must be exercised in a new way through an Office of National Economic Planning. This agency must be in a position to perceive our country's economic and social needs now and for many years to come and to provide the public, Congress, and the executive branch with alternative plans of action—not only to enable us to avert hardship and disasters, but to guide the economy in a direction consistent with our national values and goals.[3]

The general approach toward planning taken by the Initiative Committee was embodied in a bill, the Balanced Growth and Economic Planning Act of 1975, introduced in May 1975 by Senator Hubert Humphrey (Democrat of Minnesota) and Senator Jacob Javits (Republican of New York). The bill calls for establishing an Economic Planning Board in the Executive Office of the President to prepare and submit a six-year plan to Congress every two years; empowering the Joint Economic Committee of Congress to analyze the plan, hold hearings on it, consult state and local governments, and advise Congress on its adoption, modification or rejection; and identifying the nation's economic and social goals.

During the eight conferences in 1974–75 that are the primary source of our reporting, a minority of business leaders —perhaps 10 percent of those participating—spoke sympathetically about the need for business participation in national economic planning.

Business must *participate more actively in the process of setting economic and social goals for the country. It must* insist *that Congress and the Administration establish long-term, ten-year realistic goals and objectives in the vital segments of our society that are compatible with our*

*economic means. I am convinced that any realistic level
established as a goal for our "quality of life" can be
achieved, as long as there is a general understanding and
agreement within our society that such long-term targets
must be within our economic means.*

*We need a new organization to make national projections,
to decide the gap between our expectations and resources.
Once goals are set, reliance should be placed on the private
sector.*

*We have corporate planning, but we have resisted a
government planning agency. Perhaps we need a quasi-
independent agency to get government and business input.*

These proposals essentially address themselves to two problems: the instability of government economic policy and the need to appraise government spending policies more critically and carefully.

Business proposals to improve data collection, anticipate future needs and problems, provide better estimates of the costs of government policies and programs are a more sophisticated version of the common corporate belief that misunderstanding and ignorance are at the root of economic difficulties. Arjay Miller, former president of the Ford Motor Company and now dean of the Stanford Business School, was one of the first to lay out the "informational" case for planning:

Estimate the general magnitude of future increases in national output—in other words, how much new money will be available for spending.

Project the cost of presently established programs—education, health care, roads and so on—over a 10-year period.

Publish annually a listing of all our national goals, together with estimated costs and the resources available to meet them.

It is unrealistic today to contend that business must be free to pursue its own goals without reference to the broader needs and aims of the total society. All of us in business must recognize and accept the necessity for an expanded government role in our economic life. We must make the most of the situation by cooperating fully in setting the new ground rules.[4]

More recently, Robert V. Roosa, who served as Under Secretary of the Treasury before becoming an investment banker, appeared before a Congressional committee weighing the case for national planning legislation. After analyzing postwar economic developments, he commented:

The need in the United States is not, of course, for a planned economy. That, as Herbert Stein has so rightly said, articulates detailed targets, sector by sector, and seems inherently to degenerate into an undemocratic process. What we need instead is economic planning, a distinction made emphatically clear by John D. Rockefeller III. To me, planning includes procedures for evaluating longer run potentials and priorities and for bringing such evaluations to bear on present commitments; or alternatively, projecting the longer run implications of presently contemplated courses of action, and appraising those implications. The heart of planning, as

I see it, is looking ahead—taking account of the future implications of what we are contemplating or doing now, and
searching for the possible future developments that we ought
to be taking into account now. Whatever the procedures, or
the substantive implications, they must grow out of, and be
consistent with, the lasting traditions, the economic mores,
of the country concerned. For that reason, interesting and
instructive though their experience may be, I see no place
here for copying with any marked resemblance the "indica-
tive planning" of France, nor the "consensus programming"
of Japan, nor the directed, mixed economics of some
Scandinavian and other countries. I do take it as given,
though, that government will be a continuing participant and
intruder in any nation's economic life. To assume otherwise
is, I believe, utopian and of little use in developing a realistic
strategy for the future. Part of my hope for planning is that
it will make that Government involvement in the United
States more orderly, consistent and far-seeing.[5]

National planning is seen by some businessmen as a way
of making government policy more consistent over time and
less vulnerable to shifting public pressures and whims. Once
the long-range objectives have been established, "corporations
will have something to aim at and plan for," as one conference participant put it.

The most explicit proposal for dealing institutionally with
this problem is that of Fletcher Byrom, chairman of the
Koppers Corporation, who has called for a new constitutional
convention that would provide longer terms for the President
and Congress, in order to put corporate and government
policies and goals in a similar time frame.

I think we are long overdue for a serious examination and major overhaul of our system of government. I believe our political institutions are completely irrelevant to today's society.[6]

In a *Wall Street Journal* article on May 15, 1975 ("Is the Economy Sliding Into Five or Ten Years of Stagnation, Unrest?"), James P. Gannon quoted Mr. Byrom as saying:

I see the potential for significant improvement in our economy, but I don't think it will be realized. In five to 10 years, we will be moving strongly in the direction of state control of capital-intensive industries. It is already too late for the electric utilities. Our political system just won't allow corporations to make the profits they need.

Look, we've got a political system that won't work. A Congressman has to get reelected every two years. The time frames of our office holders are incompatible with the problems we face. We keep proceeding with ad hoc responses to crises. We're basically escapists. We don't want to admit we have an energy problem, so even now we still don't have an energy policy in this country.

Mr. Gannon comments:

His solution is sweeping: a constitutional convention to redefine the goals of U.S. society, overhaul the political system (perhaps a one-term, nine-year presidency and longer terms for Congressmen) and establish an economic planning body to set long-term policies.

Mr. Byrom rejects the notion he's a pessimist.

I think we're in terrible trouble, but I'm suggesting we have a way out. The system has to be changed. I see no other way. The only concern I have is whether or not we have enough time.

Improving data collection and pricing alternative national goals are possible solutions to the dual challenge of preserving the economic basis of a privately owned enterprise system while recognizing that the corporate community is no longer in a position to "set social goals by itself." As one executive argued:

> *Most businessmen don't want to include politicians in their deliberations—the politicians are considered an irritant, have different constituencies. Yet unless we incorporate them, not only will we lack legitimacy, but our goals will be unrealistic.*

He was arguing that, in effect, a joint business-public goals commission would institutionalize and legitimize corporate power—while preserving a larger role for free markets.

The Case Against Planning

Yet many businessmen—an overwhelming majority of those at the 1974–75 conferences—fear that, in whatever mild and constructive-sounding form it comes, national economic planning will inexorably lead to greater governmental control of business.

Resource planning may be the cutting edge.

The more business agrees to accept public or government guidance in determining economic policy, the more "legitimate" business may become—but the greater will be the danger that policy decisions will no longer reflect business needs.

The weaker or more abstract the nature of business-government goal setting, the less likely it will have an substantive impact on national or corporate policy. How can business give the government the power to "discipline" the society and business without confronting the possibility that governmental power might be turned against it?

Setting long-term national goals is an inherently ambiguous enterprise; it can be seen as a device by conservatives to limit government regulation and public social programs, or it can be used by liberals to weaken the autonomy of the private sector. Merely seeking to determine "what we can afford as a nation" does not say anything about whether to restrict snowmobile or automobile production (as environmentalists would want) or slow the growth of social expenditures (as most businessmen would prefer). Businessmen are fearful that they would lose more than they would gain in a planning environment, and they see the uncoordinated market as their protector—even within government. The inconsistency of government policies is not simply a matter of administrative inefficiency; it is one of the most cherished and deeply ingrained characteristics of American political life.[7] Public authority in the United States is unusually fragmented. The relative autonomy of each governmental agency mirrors the competitive anarchy of the market. To make government policies more consistent, many businessmen suspect, would require a centralization of political power that few of them would want to endorse.

It is fair to say that the overwhelming sentiment of the business community, both at the conferences and stated elsewhere for the record, is decidedly hostile to national economic planning.

Thomas A. Murphy, chairman of General Motors, was quoted in *The New York Times* of June 24, 1975, as saying:

> Sooner or later the Government plan, if it is going to serve any purpose at all, is going to mandate a different mix of goods and services than the free market would spontaneously provide. In other words, inevitably someone—maybe all of us—would lose our freedom.

In a statement to the Joint Economic Committee on November 13, 1975, Mr. Murphy elaborated on his theme, indicating that in his belief the vitality of our democracy and its demonstrated record of strength derive importantly from two convictions:

> The first is that there are clear limits to the role of government. In debating the proper role of government in a free society, few, if any, would dispute the need for government to establish the rules of conduct essential to social stability. No one denies the need for laws defining rights and duties where the unrestricted freedom of one person can seriously impinge on the rights of others. . . . In our own business, for example, standards in areas such as vehicle emissions are necessary to assure the quality of the air. But the areas in which one individual's free choice unduly impairs the rights of others are far more limited than advocates of centralized planning generally are willing to admit.

The second conviction that has strengthened our democracy is that competitive markets and free consumer choice could be relied on to set an economic course which would maximize human welfare. The individual citizen has great capacity to modify his consumption patterns through free markets. If he does not like one product, he can choose any of several other possibilities—or none at all. It well may be that what he chooses would not be what a government planner would choose for him. However, the market result does have the virtue of relying on the composite of many individual choices to identify the resources required.

This sensitive tailoring of productive resources to the complex and diverse preferences of people, expressed through free markets, is a fundamental, though often underappreciated characteristic of our system. Each consumer, given his free choice, can purchase those products which he feels most suit his own special needs and resources. Unlike the political system, every person can win in an economic "election."

On the other hand, Mr. Murphy finds that proponents of government economic planning seem to be motivated by two distinct but related notions. And he continued his statement to the Committee:

First, there is a school of thought that argues that because competitive markets do not function in all cases in the way simplistic, theoretical models of competition postulate, the system does not work at all. I submit this is pure nonsense. Second, there are those who, while not denying that the market works, do not like the choices consumers make. They are quick to apply labels such as "wasteful" or "frivolous" to these choices. This is a position held by those who believe it is only their value system or their priorities that should determine and identify the proper allocation of society's resources.

As one who has spent a lifetime in a business which must compete every day of the year to satisfy the consumer, I reject both of these notions. Government planning which goes beyond establishing the rules by which civilized people live, or which imposes value judgments on the freely functioning market, reduces economic efficiency and restricts personal freedom. Government must establish the rules of the game; it should not take part in the play.

Many participants at The Conference Board sessions put their objections to national planning in more homely terms:

Russia has a plan.

Our goal should be to allow each of us to set our own goals.

Our free enterprise system will change if we let government play too great a role in capital allocation. It is ominous for business to consider a planning board.

Corporate compensation is much higher than government compensation. We will get $35,000 worth of quality with government planning, if that is all that is paid—and that is not a top-notch planner.

The people who would do the planning are the same people who got us into the current mess.

Businessmen are, by and large, wary of some forms of data collection. They sense that "information is power," and also recognize that statistics are not self-explanatory. In the absence of whys and wherefores, many, if not most, will resist yielding a degree of power over their future to a planning institution that they perceive as increasingly vulnerable to the demands of political forces actually or potentially hostile to them.

The very time when planning appears most needed to resolve the tensions of capitalism is the time when those tensions make executives most anxious about further inroads on their autonomy. Most businessmen fear that centralizing economic direction and control over private industry would exacerbate, not lessen, political conflict. Planning, they suspect, would also intensify business competition for political favors; all industries would come to function on the model of the airlines, the defense industries, the railroads, gas pipelines, and other regulated industries, dependent on government approval for every critical decision.

The sort of pressure that many companies felt—and succumbed to—from the Nixon Administration to make illegal political contributions tends to make the business community as a whole leery of becoming more dependent upon politicians and public officials. American business leaders generally are afraid that if they were locked into an increasingly close relationship with government, it would be the political chiefs that would come out on top.

If the priorities of the government on the allocation of capital exactly mirrored those of the marketplace, planning would be pointless. If capital decisions were made on the basis of social criteria different from those of the market, some firms and industries that currently remain financially viable would suffer. What is good for the country might be perceived as markedly different from what is good for General Motors—and GM could scarcely be expected to submit to such a verdict. (It should be noted, however, that in lending support to the multibillion-dollar national highway trust fund, General Motors and other auto manufacturers were not simply "trusting to the market.")

But business executives consider that it is one thing for a particular firm to seek government help or subsidy but quite another for the business community as a whole to accept a system of planning that would violate its two most treasured values: freedom of enterprise and efficiency. Any form of planning or state capitalism beyond simple data collection would thus go against traditions very deep in the business community.

Executives are not against planning at the "micro" level; their corporations routinely plan. They are not even against national goal-setting, provided this process is not "publicized." They acknowledge that business, in quest of profits, helped establish many of the nation's current goals.

No one ever decided it, but the nation does have the goal to give every American a car and a home.

What they do not want are goals and plans decided apart from the individual profit-oriented desires of each firm, subject to the command (or at least the assent) of the market.

From the perspective of most businessmen, planning would weaken the authority of corporate management, undermine the ethos of the American version of capitalism, increase political tension within the business community, and open up the accumulation process to political pressures that business organizations might be unable to control.

Planning and the Left

The business community's skepticism about national planning is shared by the anti-corporate left. The proposals for economic planning that have periodically surfaced in the United States since the National Recovery Administration have traditionally been associated with the liberal community. Most of the current planning proposals bear a resemblance to the National Resources Planning Board, which functioned between 1933 and 1943 and played a fairly important role in collecting material on a wide variety of national issues, including city planning, urban land policies, technology, private and public research, population trends, energy resources, consumer behavior, and housing and transportation problems. The Board was killed by a conservative Congress after World War II, but the idea of national planning continued to be advocated by old New Dealers such as Leon Keyserling and Rexford Tugwell in the 1950's, and by more recent liberal critics of corporate power such as Professors Robert Engler, Michael Reagan, and Bertram Gross through the mid-sixties.[8]

However, one of the most important political legacies of the political upheaval of the mid-sixties was the disillusionment with government of some important sectors of the liberal community. The state, which for over a generation had been identified with the progressivism of the New Deal, came, under impetus of the Vietnam War, to be seen not as a countervailing force to the power of the corporation, but rather as its partner or even its agent. For example, Professor Andrew Hacker of the City University of New York wrote in 1971:

> As matters currently stand, the government does not even deserve to be called the executive committee of the bourgeoisie. Rather, it is . . . a subsidiary branch of the corporate community.[9]

While a number of prominent liberals and democratic socialists including Wassily Leontief, Leonard Woodcock, Arthur Schlesinger, Jr., Robert Lekachman, Robert Heilbroner, and John Kenneth Galbraith, have supported national economic planning, many who publicly identify themselves as hostile to the continued development and growth of corporate capitalism have greeted talk of national planning on the liberal model with skepticism or cynicism about the political and social trustworthiness of more powerful government, grown out of a period recorded in the Pentagon Papers and the Watergate tapes. The concern of the anti-corporate left is that, given the political power of business, planning will simply be used to "guide [government policy] in the interests of the capitalist class," rather than as "a route to more economic democracy and less corporate oligarchy in the United States." [10] From that perspective, the relevant issue is not whether there shall be planning, but who shall do it. The anti-capitalist left is confident that planning will be used by pro-business liberals to stabilize the capitalist system and coordinate government policy more effectively in the interests of corporations, as has been done in Western Europe; the trade unions may be co-opted, as in West Germany, to strengthen the hands of the capitalists.

Another criticism from the left is based on the argument that the problem with planning is that it is basically impossible. The editors of *Monthly Review,* for example, in the April 1975 "Review of the Month" commented on the possibilities of drawing up plans on paper that would solve a multitude of social problems. But they concluded that:

It is precisely paper dreams of this kind that dazzle our well-intentioned planners. They forget to ask where all these incredibly wasteful and absurd irrationalities came from in the first place, and they overlook the stubborn fact that each and every one of them is the fortress or hiding place of vested interests which wield enormous political power and have absolutely no intention of making the least sacrifice for the common good, even if that somewhat elusive concept is defined wholly in capitalist terms.

The ideologies of business and its harshest anti-capitalist critics are in ironic contradiction: most businessmen oppose planning because it will *strengthen* the power of forces hostile to the business corporation, while many members of the left are suspicious of "capitalist" economic planning for precisely the opposite reason: that it will *weaken* the forces hostile to corporate power.

Preserving Corporate Autonomy

Virtually all businessmen would like to restrict and, if possible, reduce government interference in their own business affairs. To be sure, as government expenditures mounted to the hundreds of billions of dollars, with much of this money going to business firms, there was an element of hypocrisy in the attitude of many businessmen toward government spending. Strangely enough, some of the strongest business champions of "free enterprise" have been in the defense sector, largely or wholly dependent on government spending, for which they have lobbied strongly. And many businessmen in regulated industries, while decrying regulation, have actually been the leading proponents of regulation because of the protections or subsidies it affords their own companies. At a 1975 conference on the Ford Administration's efforts to reform (and reduce) government regulation of business, Roderick Hills, then a White House counselor to the President and subsequently chairman of the Securities and Exchange Commission, observed:

> The obvious problem of regulatory agencies is that they have protected the industries they are regulating, not the consumers. . . . The government has unwittingly created governmental monopoly where no monopoly existed, and they have acted in far too many cases to protect the industries themselves. When these bills to reform the regulatory agencies go to Congress, our biggest problems are going to be those industries that we are trying to restore to the free enterprise system.[11]

It has always been awkward, to put it mildly, for the business community to speak out against excessive government spending and regulation, and then for particular firms to request government help the moment economic difficulties struck. It was an embarrassment with which, however, corporate executives have managed to live. However, the gloomy long-range economic forecasts as well as the rather tarnished image of business have in recent years clearly left their mark. When business demands for government aid show signs of becoming endemic—as they now appear to executives—then there is the need for the business community to think seriously about the long-term implications of its strategy. There has been growing resentment toward those business firms that have gone to the government for "bail-outs."

> *Each business wants some part of the governmental pie for its particular business, yet no one cares about the effect of these demands on the total picture of business-government relations.*
>
> *I'm upset about business going to Washington for help. Each firm looks out for its short-term interest and then complains about government becoming too big and powerful.*
>
> *Business has to try to keep its members from going to Washington. We must find a way of staying out of government's pockets.*
>
> *When we are in trouble, we ask government for help and planning.*

It is unlikely that most businessmen adequately appreciate the significance of this position. One of the critical problems facing the U.S. economy is the considerable rigidity introduced by the massive size and economic importance of large firms. It would certainly take extraordinary courage for the government to refuse to come to the aid of a major firm on the verge of bankruptcy—and face the attendant loss of jobs and income. This was what swung government support to the Lockheed Aircraft Corporation—a considerable embarrassment to the conservative Ford Administration when it was refusing to "bail out" New York City in 1975.

Opposition to government aid for failing companies, however, is less than firm among businessmen. Yet, in principle, they warmly agree with the doctrine enunciated by William Simon, Secretary of the Treasury:

> . . . if you believe in a free marketplace and in the right to succeed in business, you also must accept the other side of the coin; the right to go out of business. . . . I believe that if companies fail to adapt to changes in competitive conditions . . . they have no claim to public support . . . the public should not be fleeced of taxes to keep any business alive that, like the dinosaur, has outlived its usefulness.[12]

Business may depart from its anti-government ideology occasionally to cope with a truly felt crisis—a war, or even the inflation of 1971, which businessmen blamed on the rapid escalation of wage rates. They supported Mr. Nixon's use of wage-price controls as a means of "zapping" labor, as price controller Arnold Weber put it. But whatever reductions in wage rates took place were evidently not worth the administrative and political difficulties for business in the longer run. They demanded that controls be ended as 1972 wore on— and so they were, after the November 1972 election.[13] The relationship of business to the National Recovery Act in the early Roosevelt years reveals a similar pattern: original corporate enthusiasm followed by disappointment and disillusionment.

Businessmen are by no means against reforms that would make government programs more coherent and consistent, and that would force Congress and the bureaucracy to be aware of the economic costs of what they do; such reforms have been enacted with the support of business. The new Congressional budget-review procedure is an outstanding example. The issue is really one of degree: Will these mechanisms encourage or discourage more government spending? Will they strengthen corporate autonomy or weaken it? In short, what impact will they have on the locus of economic decision-making?

Executives lack confidence in central decision-making, yet they very much want governmental policies to be predictable and economically sound and consistent: They want the government to plan better for itself, but not for them.

There is a difference between a planned society and one that plans.

CHAPTER FOUR

How Business Views Its Critics

The world is laying all its ills at the feet of business.

HOW DO CORPORATE EXECUTIVES explain the low repute into which business has fallen in recent years? Some blame the performance on business itself—or at least on too many individual companies that have violated laws or proper ethical standards. They feel that the public has every right to be concerned about instances of deteriorating product quality, merger manipulations, business frauds such as those of Penn Central and Equity Funding, the uncertain quality and sometimes misleading character of corporate accounting— and the undependability of professional auditing of corporate accounts, the erratic performance of the stock market, the overextension of business and banking debt in the frenetic race for growth, the high rate of business failures and the demand of corporations in trouble for government bail-outs, the contribution of business itself to the national slump, inflation, declining living standards, unemployment. Particularly shocking to public confidence in business, some executives recognize, have been the scandals of illegal corporate

102

campaign contributions in the 1972 Presidential election campaign and subsequent evidence of business bribery of public officials at home and abroad.

A few participants in the closed conferences were sharply critical of the behavior of many of their fellow businessmen. As one put it:

> *To my mind, business has earned a fair share of its deteriorating social image. Excesses in advertising, quality deterioration, abuses of SEC, merger manipulations, the hell-with-the-public attitude, inexcusable cases of fraud, stock manipulations have all contributed to the notion that there is something wrong with business, its judgments, and its ethics. Business has been tarred and feathered by these individuals and businesses who want to turn the profit free enterprise system into a spoils and greed system.*

This opinion, however, is decidedly a minority one among executives. While all recognize that it is possible to cite numerous examples of recent corporate misconduct, very few regard these as the "root cause" of the disenchantment of the public with business. The overwhelming majority feel that the institutions they lead have performed their economic role more than adequately and that the evidence that has recently surfaced about business malfeasance represents deviations from the norm of executive behavior and business conduct; it does not represent the norm.

Watergate and the illegal business contributions that helped finance the Nixon election campaign were mentioned infrequently and usually only to attribute the scandal to "human nature":

Watergate reflects how people operate under stress.

A survey of executives representing top and middle management conducted in the summer of 1973 by the Opinion Research Corporation reported that 47 percent believed that "the standards of the individuals involved, rather than the administration or party" was "at the base of the behavior that has been revealed by Watergate," and 37 percent contended that the behavior reflected "long-standing practice in politics."

Businessmen feel that there is "nothing new" about what happened during the Nixon Administration—either in terms of corporate contributions or the misuse of authority and government agencies, such as the CIA or the FBI, by an administration to harass its "enemies." Since most businessmen feel that their own performance has not deteriorated, they attribute the low status of business in the public-opinion polls to a failure of communication on their part and deliberate distortion by "the media."

Poor Communications

If one theme dominates the concerns of business executives these days, it is their inability to communicate adequately with the public. It is hard to exaggerate the importance executives attach to this problem. More than any other— including the resource scarcity, inflation, unemployment, the capital shortage, the decline of business political impact— the failure of communications is defined as the basic threat to the enterprise system. Its solution is held critical to solving all other business problems: If only the public understood how the business system operates, particularly the critical role of profits, public policy would become more responsible and the ability of business to survive and fulfill its economic and social obligations would be assured. But the public lacks the knowledge to make an informed judgment about the role of business. As one executive put it:

> *Business leaders will not be permitted a role in forming social goals. We are suspect because we represent a system that is no longer understood. Profit, the very foundation of our economic wealth, has become a dirty word.*

Other typical sentiments were:

> *The most vigorous critic understands us least.*

> *Public acceptance of business has reached its lowest ebb in many a generation.*

> *Understanding comes before appreciation. The whole world is in a bad mood.*

> *The public doesn't believe us and when it distrusts us, it turns to government for protection. Business must gain the trust of the public.*

Executives seem *personally,* not just politically or economically, concerned about their low public esteem; one gets the impression that they would be just as upset even if they were convinced that public disfavor had no adverse policy impact. The chief executives of corporations constitute America's upper class. Unlike the upper classes of precapitalist societies, they are not a leisure class; they feel that they are competent and creative people upon whose judgment and effort rests the economic welfare of millions of individuals in this country and all over the globe. They regard their high financial rewards and privileged lives—both on and off the job—as the consequences of their great contributions to productivity.

That far more of the recreation of top executives is business-related than of any other occupational group may not be simply a result of the rules of the Internal Revenue Service. Whether in the boardroom, or at the Greenbrier or at Pebble Beach, or in Paris or Rio, they are "working," thinking up projects or putting together deals that will enrich themselves and benefit others as well.

The gap that has developed between their self-image and their public image is especially galling and disturbing to American businessmen. The American businessman has traditionally been held in higher esteem than his counterparts in any other nation. Unlike the European bourgeoisie, which has had to struggle for social recognition against the bitter opposition of the aristocracy (a struggle that is still far from won) the top businessmen in America historically confronted no other social or political elite. They did not go through a period of public disapproval as a result of their challenge to the *ancien régime*.

Yet there is another dynamic at work. American "egalitarianism," the belief that all men have equal rights and equal opportunities and that anyone who is clever enough or energetic enough or lucky enough can get to the top, produces an elite that is apt to be unusually insecure about its standing. The ability of everyone to "make it" means that no one has ever "got it made"—the expression itself is ironic. Success is a daily process, not an end. Money is admittedly something, but it is far from everything; American businessmen don't want to "sit on their assets."

For most executives, fame and immortality are beyond reach. In a business civilization there seems to be no place for permanent status: the only relevant standard for judgment is the last quarter's earnings. A vibrant business system cannot be satisfied with the past performance of its leaders. In that sense, there is something a bit sad about *Fortune* magazine's recently established "Business Hall of Fame." In commenting on it, Max Ways notes that most businessmen, even when they achieve public recognition, are usually recognized for their nonbusiness achievements, i.e., "statesmen" (George Washington), "inventors" (Eli Whitney, Thomas Edison), or "philanthropists" (Peter Cooper). Ways suggests that the contemporary problem is compounded by the nature of business leadership: "The old-style leader was clearly visible, lifted far above his collaborators." [1] Today, by contrast, Professor Fouraker of the Harvard Business School comments: "Visibility for chief executives has almost always been associated with disasters." There are relatively few heroes in the business community. Most "businessmen would prefer to remain anonymous." [2]

Oddly enough, the pervasive business values—values that emphasize change and performance today and tomorrow—make the executive feel unappreciated for his past efforts. As one executive noted, we have fewer and fewer corporations that bear their managers' or founders' names. Executives nowadays have only a short spell at the top—five or six years, typically. What distinguishes the current generation of top executives from the previous two or three is their anonymity. During the era of the muckrakers and down through the 1930's, hostility to business had a strong personal dimension. The men who dominated American business in the latter half of the nineteenth century—such figures as John D. Rockefeller, J. P. Morgan, Cornelius Vanderbilt, Andrew Carnegie, Jim Fisk, Jay Gould—were well known to their contemporaries. Today, the names of the chief executive officers of corporations that have been most heavily in the public spotlight—one thinks of the executives of the major oil companies—are virtually unknown to the general public. Said one executive:

> *The oil companies have done a great job; they deserve a medal.*

Regardless of the merits of this assessment, America, being a thoroughly bourgeois society, has no equivalent of the Queen's honor list; thanks to the success of our revolution, we have no aristocratic honors to bestow for distinguished pecuniary performance. The only "medal" we have to bestow is the applause of the financial community at the increase in earnings reported each quarter, and that recognition, as every executive knows, is rather ephemeral.

The Press as Culprit

The business community feels extremely hostile these days toward the press and the electronic media, which it blames for the low public esteem of business. No one theme was so consistently mentioned at every conference, and few themes enjoyed such unanimous support.

Executives are firmly convinced that "a majority of citizens would support the free enterprise system if they understood it," and that the press denies the public that knowledge.

> *What good is it to have a story to tell if the media won't let you tell it?*

Business believes the press wields great power to shape public opinion and constitutes a "virtual fourth branch of government." But its power, many businessmen believe, is consistently used to "defame those in authority, promote dissension and political division," and "to use the poor performance of a few to castigate the entire business community."

> *Even though the press is a business, it doesn't reflect business values.*
>
> *The press is forever at war with the creative minds of free men.*
>
> *Unless the press stops tearing down our system and begins to tell the public how it works, business leaders will not be permitted any future participation in the formation of social goals.*
>
> *The media are destructive and misinformed.*

The resignation of Richard Nixon has deeply traumatized many business executives. While quite a few feel that their trust in Nixon was betrayed, many nevertheless feel that he was "hounded out of office" by his political enemies in the media—and that all business was smeared and hurt in the process. Many businessmen fear that the end result of their financial support for Nixon's successful reelection campaign effort was the election in 1974 of a Congress hostile to business and a public antipathy to business that will take a generation to live down. While many recognize that, in retrospect, "business placed its hope on a white elephant," much of their anger is directed at the press for spitefully bringing the entire political-economic system into disrepute. They see the attack on Nixon as biased and personally vindictive. To quote a widely repeated joke: "If President Nixon had walked across the Potomac, the headline of the next morning's *Washington Post* would read, 'Richard Nixon can't swim.' "

Many conference participants put major blame for the public's misunderstanding of business on the three national television networks, especially for their refusal to allow corporations to purchase time to present their views of various public policy issues. The network news reports were often denounced as biased or malicious. The wife of one chief executive commented:

> *It makes me sick to watch the evening news night after night and see my husband and the efforts of his industry maligned.*

Even entertainers are not exempt from the bill of indictment:

One little smirk or crack on the Tonight Show biases the opinions of millions of Americans.

While oil-industry executives were strongest in their denunciation of the media for misrepresenting their role and bringing on public policies detrimental to their interests and future performance, virtually all executives found the media's treatment of the energy crisis "unfair" and "inaccurate."

The suggestion disseminated by the media that the energy shortage in 1974 was contrived by the oil industry to increase its prices and profits was generally viewed as "fantastic." That such an erroneous viewpoint could be taken seriously by so many Americans was cited by businessmen as evidence of the damage to the credibility of all business caused by powerful but irresponsible news media.

We must convince the media to play a leadership role, not to tear down our system, but to provide leadership for the public by telling them how business works.

The public doesn't set the goals, the media do. We need the media to help sell the survival system to America.

Business complaints against the media were not confined to national newspapers or television networks. A number of businessmen expressed concern about the reporting of business in their local newspapers. Several reported that their complaints about biased reporting were shared by the publishers, but that the publishers felt handicapped. One told a participant:

*The minute I try to suggest something to a reporter, he
screams "editorial freedom" and threatens to get the Guild
after me.*

Some businessmen attribute the alleged distortions of the
news media to the perpetual pursuit of sensationalism:

*How come so many shortsighted opportunists end up in
Washington? My answer is that the villains in the picture are
the news media . . . to sell the newspapers and to get people
to listen to TV and radio news, the media are forced to
accentuate the sensational, the scandalous, and the distorted.
Too often the media find it necessary to eulogize the under-
dog—the criminal. With blatant headlines, scare tactics,
subtle, slanted reporting, the media move people's minds to
make opportunistic short-term decisions. The media have
a tremendous effect on the people of this country and must
take the responsibility for the opportunistic short-term
thinking on the Washington scene.*

Businessmen believe—and in effect charge—that the
media are simply in hot pursuit of financial gain. The press
is not "venal" in the sense of accepting bribes to print what
some outside force wants—but it is interested in making
money by exploiting public interests, appetites, passions. For
most executives, all the world is a market; behind every
activity there must lie the motive of individual self-interest
and gain. It is not that publishers and reporters, producers
and editors and network executives necessarily share a sub-
versive political philosophy, but that the pursuit of their own
short-term economic gain leads them to tell the public what
it wants to hear—and that evidently includes the worst about

the business sector. In other words, the media are accused of simply "marketing" whatever best sells newspapers or boosts audience ratings.

Some outraged business executives charge that the decline in the public's confidence in business has been paralleled by the relative increase in the profits of the press and TV networks, implying that the two phenomena are perceived as interconnected. Businessmen, who feel their profits are under attack in the media, counterattack against this presumed hypocrisy. Rawleigh Warner, Jr., chairman of Mobil Oil Corporation, writes:

> The *Washington Post* said recently that the government had an "urgent" duty to correct what that paper called the "vast enrichment" of the oil companies. This offers the opportunity for an instructive comparison. The net earnings of Texaco, one of the more profitable oil companies, increased 57 per-cent between 1970 and 1973. During this same period, the net income of the Washington Post Company increased about 160 per cent.
>
> Last year Mobil's worldwide earnings were up 48 per cent over 1972. Those of the New York Times Company were up 58 per cent; of the Washington Post Company, 37 per cent. The networks also apparently had a good year in 1973.[3]

Executives also attribute the irresponsibility of the press and TV networks to the alleged ignorance of journalists. It is profoundly irritating for executives to have their decisions and motives "second-guessed" by individuals who, by the nature of their occupational role, are far less knowledgeable about the activities in the industry under attack than are the executives. They resent the assumption that an outsider is qualified to pass judgment on a firm or industry to which they have devoted most of their adult lives.

Business executives sometimes attribute jealousy, envy, and hence, meanness, to journalists, unfavorably contrasting "those who criticize" with "those who do"—meaning themselves. At one of the conferences, a businessman heatedly asked a newspaper publisher present, "Why don't you tell the truth about us?"

The publisher, just as heatedly, replied, "If we did tell the public everything we know about you, they would like you even less."

How the Press Sees It

Journalists and publishers believe that a professional press, and a genuinely free press, is bound to be a critical press. If anything, many news people feel, the press has been too *uncritical* of business, preferring to take on easier and less dangerous opponents. According to an ancient newspaper formula, it is always safe to attack the man-eating shark. Some newsmen, as well as many outside critics of the press, feel that foreign dictators, crooked politicians, and unsavory criminals (especially petty criminals) are human variants of the man-eating shark, and ask why the press does not do a deeper, more extensive and hard-hitting job of investigating business corporations that deceive and gouge the public or corrupt the political process.

The common implication or charge from these nonbusiness

critics of the press is that newspapers and television stations and networks are businesses themselves and are incapable of standing up to other businesses that are their advertisers, bankers, suppliers, and members of the same club or establishment. Such a charge strikes at least some journalists as closer to the truth than the common charge of business that the press is anti-business in a mindless, envious, hypocritical way, curries favor with the public by attacking great corporations as the authors of special-interest legislation and public policies and as corrupters of politicians and the democratic process.

It is obviously difficult for both sets of accusations—that the press is too soft on business and too hostile toward business—to be simultaneously true. If we were compelled to say which charge is more nearly right, it would be the former: Corporate actions inimical to public interests receive, in our view, too little attention, rather than too much, in the press and on the air. The problem is not necessarily one of venality on the part of the press; it is a great deal harder to keep one's eye on a multitude of businesses and to find out what is going on within them than it is to cover the federal government, foreign wars, or local crime. So vast a business scandal as the collapse of the Penn Central Railroad happened with scarcely a word of warning from the press. It was a lowly security analyst—not the large business press corps nor the New York Stock Exchange nor, for that matter, the host of federal regulators—who discovered that Equity Funding was engaged in the criminal activity of writing insurance policies on "dead souls," like Gogol's Chichikov. It was a lack of attentiveness and investigative zeal, rather than venality, that was at the root of the failure of both the press and the public watchdogs.

The problem of exposing out-and-out business crime is, however, not the heart of the issue; the real problem for the press—and the society generally—is deciding what *is* unacceptable (but not necessarily illegal) business activity. There are businessmen, as well as some professors and newspaper people, who maintain that whatever is legal is proper, even when it is in one's own interest. The law is not, in any case, a dead and frozen set of rules, but a living and evolving institution meant to serve the interests of a free and decent society. It is only by investigating and exposing technically legal activities of corporations or other special interests that the laws can be improved. The press considers that its job is to serve the broad public interest, not the special interests— in the words of Adolph S. Ochs, "to give the news impartially, without fear or favor, regardless of any party, sect or interest involved." [4]

Business and Intellectuals

The business community's anxiety about the attitudes of the press is part of a broader concern—that the values of the productive system and those of the society's intellectuals have become seriously out of line. While the press is a particular focus of business concern, a variety of other vehicles of public communication also disturb executives. One put it:

> *There is no good book that defends free enterprise. Movies and television screenwriters are against us and blame us for everything.*

Another recounted:

> *I asked a college professor I know to suggest a book to me*
> *that defends the free enterprise system. You know all he*
> *could suggest to me? Adam Smith!*

Everything in the personal experience of businessmen suggests to them that the values and goals around which they have organized their productive lives are appropriate to the future needs of their fellow citizens in whose economic achievements they take a great deal of pride. But they feel painfully frustrated about how to "get their views across" to the public about the economic system that they believe is responsible for national progress. Most chief executive officers are extremely well informed and articulate when it comes to discussing their product, business, or industry, but few feel they can present a convincing justification of the free enterprise system to the outside public, especially to audiences who have not shared their experiences and come to them with fundamentally different assumptions.

The division between "intellectual" and "practical" people haunts American businessmen:

> *Those whose experience enables them to understand the*
> *economic system do not have the breadth to explain it,*
> *while those who have the ability to adequately explain it*
> *are already distant from it—and thus really don't understand*
> *it.*

The gap between those who are capable of running the business system and those who wind up explaining it is most vividly expressed in the attitude of business toward the educational system. Next to the government and the media, the institution that is the most prominent focus of the hostility of business executives is the university. Since a growing proportion of Americans attend institutions of higher education, colleges and universities are seen as playing a critical role in determining the long-term future of the "free enterprise" system. Many business executives put much of the blame for the growing public dislike of business on the bias of college and university faculties:

> *A large portion of our educational faculties throughout America have an anti-establishment bias.*

> *There is no comparison between free enterprise and other systems if they understand the facts. But few young people know what free enterprise means. That's why they don't like it.*

> *The young know more about the Cuban and Chinese systems than they do about ours. Students are being deprived of a freedom of choice. They don't know how our system works, so how can they choose it?*

> *How did we let the educational system fail the free enterprise system? Where did we go wrong?*

Although businessmen are critical of the universities and colleges, particularly of the liberal arts faculties' attitudes toward business, they continue to support higher education. Even during the "campus revolutions" of the late sixties, when many of them were very critical of the permissiveness of faculties and administrations, business leaders continued to give both their time (as trustees, visitors, etc.) and their money to the very institutions they were denouncing.

Few executives complain about the quality of education in graduate and undergraduate schools of business. Without exception, businessmen appear pleased with the ability, knowledge, and motivation of their own junior executives. Top executives at the conferences frequently expressed admiration for the educational preparation of their younger managers.

There was some concern expressed about the leftward bias of economics professors. One executive contended that "nineteen out of the top twenty graduate departments of economics are hostile to free enterprise." (The exception was said to be the University of Chicago.) However, the economists appeared to receive less blame for the miseducation of the young than "social scientists," especially sociologists.

The social scientists via government play a decisive role in creating social definitions that are improper. We shouldn't accept Ph.D.s' definitions of what we do.

It is not a coincidence that the initials of behavioral science are b.s.

There are no more intellectual conservatives.

Executives offer no common explanation as to why social scientists are hostile to business; some simply assert it, while the more frequent view is to attribute it to ignorance:

Sociologists simply don't know economics.

At one conference it was suggested that university faculties, like the media, may not be immune from the enticements of the market:

Professors may say things critical of business in their class-rooms as a way of increasing course enrollment.

There seems to be a widespread feeling among businessmen that the university system has had its loyalties captured by forces hostile to the business system and that this accounts for much of the public's misunderstanding of business. Several executives offered stories of their children's educational experience to confirm the effectiveness of the anti-free enterprise spirit of university faculties.

The business community's worries about higher education are not confined to well-known centers of dissident opinion such as Berkeley, Harvard, and Columbia; businessmen are also anxious about the so-called "backwater schools," local and regional institutions. Many executives are concerned that more and more schools are moving from the private to the public sector for their main source of support because of financial pressures. They see this as a trend eroding the support for business:

The system of higher education is becoming increasingly public. State employees are not going to be teaching the free enterprise system. What can you expect of state employees?

College professors are doubtless more "liberal" than the American electorate generally, though few are socialists or communists. However, for businessmen to hold professors solely responsible for the low esteem in which business is held by many young people implies a degree of faculty influence over the political views of students that seems vastly inflated. For whatever reason, polls over a period of time indicate that college students are, in fact, more liberal than the population as a whole and more critical of business. Gallup reports that only 20 percent of college students interviewed believe that business executives have high moral and ethical standards, and 87 percent believe that business is more concerned with profit than with public responsibility.[5] One Harris poll indicated that 74 percent of college students were in favor of government regulation of business, compared with 54 percent of the total population.[6] This difference in attitudes may reflect the political content of classroom instruction less than it does the very nature of a liberal arts education. Higher education probably does—and should—encourage a generally more critical attitude toward established values and institutions. Scholars and journalists worth their salt value this independence and their right to pursue the truth, wherever it may lead; they do not readily submit to higher authority, and their values are basically nonhierarchical or anti-hierarchical.

The values of both the university and the press frequently bring its members into conflict with the established authorities in both business and government. This is, or ought to be, a healthy tension; a society is free when each of its major institutions reflects a diversity of outlooks and viewpoints. The degree to which college faculty members, or journalists, or other groups of citizens are able to question and examine the virtues and performance of those "in power" can function as a check on the abuse of power. Sometimes it is simply a "disturbance of the peace"—a peace that has become tedious, boring, and stagnant to those challenging it.

In their mistrust of higher education, some business executives betray a certain anti-intellectualism, an attitude that has deep roots in the American tradition. As the classic American joke has it, "If you're so smart, why ain't you rich?" Anti-intellectualism, as opposed to hostility to educational institutions, has always been a part of the business tradition. The historian Thomas Cochran, writes:

> Professors, ministers, and literary men are held to be impractical and likely to have theories dangerous to social stability.
> This anti-intellectual attitude has been strong ever since the later nineteenth century. Merle E. Curti, a leading scholar of American thought, notes that "American respect for business, and the businessman's inadequate appreciation of the intellectual, have, by tradition, been pretty generally taken for granted." Thus, the businessman has been able to a degree to live in his part of the culture by his own precepts, regarding other beliefs as unimportant to the main task at hand, the material improvement of the nation.[7]

When the "intellectual" enters the government and begins to play a role in policy—a post-Depression phenomenon—the two (government bureaucrats and professors) merge, in the opinion of business people.

Paradoxically, the common business perception of the university as hostile to business is the opposite of that held by those few students and faculty members who do consider themselves opposed to capitalism. One of the major contentions of the student movement of the 1960's was that the university was united with government and business, and was an integral part of the "establishment" or the "system." To support their views these radical critics cited the critical role of the university in training workers for corporations, its acceptance of research contracts with business or government, its effectiveness in tracking students of various socioeconomic backgrounds into their "appropriate positions" in the occupational hierarchy, its financial dependence on the growth and profitability of corporations through endowment funds and investments, and its fundamentally conservative role in instructing students in the dominant values of the society, including the importance of competition, the "myth" of democratic control of the political process, the belief that success is a function of one's efforts. The radicals contend that the lack of discussion of viable systematic alternatives to capitalism shows that the institutional division between business and the university is primarily a matter of convenience, and that the occasional clashes between these institutions are trivial or "bureaucratic."

With their strong emphasis on vocational training, American universities are doubtless more business-oriented than universities abroad. In specific areas businessmen are well aware of the importance of the universities to them—not only as training grounds for their professionals but as research centers.

Nevertheless, many businessmen remain unhappy over the failure of American higher education—or lower education, for that matter—to teach young people greater respect for and loyalty to the American system. One business executive, recounting his visit to a primary school in Communist China, said:

A little child, probably no more than three years old, came up to me, stuck his fist near my mouth and said something very angry to me. I asked the translator what he said, and

*she translated: "The people will be victorious over the
running-dog imperialists." Now, why don't our young people
feel that identification with our system?*

Clashing Conceptions

The conflict between business executives and their journal-
istic and academic critics appears to be rooted in fundamentally different conceptions of their roles and philosophies. One
university president told the story of a businessman serving
on his advisory board who made the professorial members of
that board furious by constantly referring to them as "employees" of the university. Similarly, businessmen are baffled
or enraged by the inability of publishers of news media to
control their editorial staffs. The relative autonomy of both
faculty members and reporters simply has no counterpart in
the typical business organization. In the old days business
hierarchical and managerial prerogatives could be and usually
were applied (and, though sometimes resisted, were rarely
ridiculed) in both the academic and the newspaper world.

With the passage of time, both academic institutions and
the press have gained a far greater degree of independence
from the control of property owners and businessmen, and
with that independence has come an intensified clash between
academics and journalists on one side and businessmen and
government officials on the other. The well-known sociologist
Seymour Martin Lipset has observed:

> The impression that the core of the intellectual and the com-
> munications world is hostile to the managerial components
> of society has been sustained by a variety of opinion surveys.

These show that among those employed in such work, the more socially critical, the ones who most strongly reject the status quo, are most likely to come from the most successful. Research by Everett Ladd and myself indicates that the most influential within the university world, those who are in the most prestigious universities, who have achieved the most as scholars, are most disposed to a critical *Weltanschauung*. . . . The more prestigious the newspaper or broadcast medium, the more socially critical its editors, culture critics, and reporters. A survey of the opinions of 500 leaders of American life conducted in 1971–72 found that those in the media—publishers, editors, television executives, and columnists—were the most "anti-establishmentarian" of all groups interviewed. Solid majorities of the "media leaders" supported the youth rebellion and expressed a lack of confidence in the country's major social and political institutions.[8]

The leaders of the academic and communications worlds believe, however, that it is a serious mistake for businessmen to suppose that the real troubles of the American society stem from the role they have been playing as observers, investigators, and critics, rather than from real social and political events. Katharine Graham, publisher of the *Washington Post*, recently told a group of businessmen:

It is, of course, very human to credit or blame the messenger for the nature of the news. I suspect that the classic complaint—Why does the press always report what's wrong?—is as old as the very notion of an independent press. These days, however, I hear a variation of that question constantly and with increasing animus. It usually is put something like this: Now that the press has torn down a President, isn't it your duty to build the country up and help restore national confidence? . . .

Our job, however comprehensive, is quite sharply limited. It is limited to describing the world as it actually is, not as any party or group—ourselves included—would prefer it to be. . . .

Obviously that point has not entirely gotten across. And obviously the press, like many other institutions, needs to do much better in explaining our purposes, our standards and our goals. But that does not mean that we should compromise those standards and principles in an effort to appease our critics or strike some artificial balance between good and bad news. That would not only be self-defeating; it would erode the nation's capacity to understand the trials which we are passing through, and thus to deal with them.[9]

Indeed, thus far this message has not gotten through. And, as many statements of business executives at the 1974–75 conferences made clear, an obsession with "image" continues to characterize the leadership of American business. In 1950, William H. Whyte quoted this statement:

Today's challenge, today's dire necessity, is to sell—to resell if you will—to free Americans the philosophy that has kept us and our economy free.[10]

Businessmen at the 1974–75 conferences were still saying:

We have been successful in selling products, but not ourselves.

We have been inept in the communication of ideas and the information that creates understanding among people.

CHAPTER FIVE

A Question of Legitimacy

AMERICAN BUSINESSMEN SAY they see no real conflict between their self-interest and the public interest. Profits, they
emphasize, are crucial to the achievement of the material
abundance that all Americans, regardless of their politics,
desire. And, far from being incompatible with the most
humane and decent aspirations of the society, material abundance makes those "higher" aspirations and values possible.
"First feed the face, then know right from wrong," they feel—
in the words of Bertolt Brecht, the left-wing poet—with the
basic difference that American businessmen consider that
capitalism delivers the goods and communism doesn't. But
their deep concern is that most Americans don't understand
the system they have and from which they benefit:

> *What we have is a business civilization. We must com-
> municate this fact.*

> *We are the free enterprise system. We should be proud of
> it and defend it.*

There is an element of nostalgia in those remarks—and not
just for President Calvin Coolidge who said, "The business

127

of America is business." For there was indeed a time when virtually the entire nation naturally and enthusiastically expressed the business ideology. As the English historian D. W. Brogan wrote:

> The pioneer American had a real economic as well as emotional interest in growth, in encouraging the booster spirit. If he wanted to stay in the new settlement which he had chosen, he had an interest in other people's staying too. Only so could the profitable rise in values which he counted on be realized. Only so could money be borrowed on the future prosperity of the settlement. . . . This conception of growth as everybody's business, everybody's interest, is deep-rooted in the American national psychology.[1]

Yet if "business" and the individual businessman have historically enjoyed unusual support, respect, and prestige in the United States, the status of the institution which has carried on the greater part of business activity for nearly a century has been somewhat more ambiguous. It is the corporation—and not the businessman—that has periodically confronted the challenge of justifying its crucial role in the nation's economic and political processes. To talk of the business corporation as facing a "crisis of legitimacy" does not imply that there exists any significant controversy as to whether it should exist; there is not. Rather it is to suggest that corporate leaders are being confronted with two basic questions: By what right do you who manage these huge corporations exercise your power? And what means do we have to insure that corporate power will be exercised in accord with some generally accepted notion of the public interest? The answers that business and society provide to those questions will largely determine the evolution of the American economic system.

The problem of legitimating political authority has been one of the most crucial problems for political rulers and political philosophers since the emergence of the modern nation-state in the fifteenth century. What distinguishes the modern democratic state is that it has sought to justify its authority on the basis of public *consent,* while previously the most commonly accepted basis of governmental authority was hereditary or religious—"divine right."

The problem of legitimating institutional or personal authority, however, is not confined to governmental institutions, but permeates modern Western society. It arises whenever unequal distributions of wealth and power are not simply accepted as "natural" by those who do not benefit proportionately from whatever social arrangements exist.

The Accomplishments of Business

How, then, do the contemporary leaders of American business define and defend their role, which has brought them greater wealth or power than most of their fellow citizens possess?

Corporate executives take a great deal of pride in the role they have played in American society:

> *The American free enterprise system is not perfect, yet it*
> *has produced more benefits than any other system in history.*
> *We are the healthiest, wealthiest, best educated, most*
> *generous nation in the history of the world.*

By efficiently meeting the needs of the public for goods and services, they have provided jobs and contributed to a steady increase in per capita income. Business is the "foundation of the good life in the U.S."

> *Business is truly the servant of society. Business weaves the fabric of our people. It is the bloodstream that provides the strength for our society.*

Business has more than adequately met its obligations to society and can continue to do so if given the chance. Many executives recognize, of course, that the accomplishments of a society cannot be defined exclusively in material terms. Yet they emphasize that economic accumulation—the production of goods and services—is the *sine qua non* for the achievements of any other goals:

> *A high standard of living is an essential part of a good quality of life.*

> *You can talk of the quality of life only after you have met the quantity of goods.*

An economically healthy private sector is critical to the welfare of the entire society; it is upon its productivity and strength that the viability of all other institutions rests.

> *We are like the head of a household, and the public sector is like our wife and children. They can consume only what we produce.*

Many executives resent the idea that they serve only themselves while the government or citizens' action groups serve society. One executive remarked indignantly:

> *Business is the most responsible institution by far. I resent Ralph Nader calling his organization a public service organization. My company is a public service institution.*
>
> *Critics of business claim to represent the public, but they have forgotten that business does what the public wants.*

Many business leaders are troubled that, because an increasing share of social benefits reaches the public through government agencies, the public holds government, and not business, responsible for those benefits.

> *If the public listed the benefits it has received, such as the minimum wage, paid vacations, unemployment benefits, occupational health and safety standards, environmental protection, it would place these items under government, even though business pays a significant share of them, and even in many cases initiated them.*
>
> *Laws are necessary for many things, yet government gets the credit while we pay.*

Another executive argued:

> *We are simply a funnel through which goods and services pass. There is no such thing as the regulation of business; in the final analysis the consumer pays.*
>
> *Corporations do not pay taxes, they collect them.*

In a similar vein, another suggested that business should really not attempt to shape or restrain public demands on business:

> *It is their pound of flesh, not ours.*

The legitimacy of the business role in society thus implicitly rests on the identity of the corporation's goals with the basic welfare of the society—an identity that is accounted for by the importance to society of the corporation's proven area of expertise: the creation of wealth.

The objectives of business and the achievement of social goals are the same. Without business, there is no money, no resources, no environmental protection.

We believe our goals are compatible with the best interests in society.

Given their belief in the congruence of social and corporate goals, executives generally feel every reason to take pride in their role in the development of American society. That society's expectations have now come to encompass public values and qualitative, rather than only quantitative, goals is seen by business as a mark of the corporation's extraordinary success in satisfying the public's material expectations. One executive put it:

Our problems are those of success.

Another quoted approvingly from public opinion polls that show that the public's expectations of corporate performance have come to include such aims as ameliorating the urban crisis, improving the physical environment, providing meaningful work. This man concluded that, with all the criticisms business has recently received,

When it comes to a critical problem, the public still looks to us to carry the load because deep down inside it knows that we can do the job.

In 1973, Louis Harris reviewed the change in the public's expectations of business between 1966 and 1973. He found that over three quarters of the American people agreed that "business should provide special leadership in the following areas: controlling air and water pollution, 92 percent; eliminating economic depressions, 88 percent; rebuilding our cities, 85 percent; enabling people to use their talents creatively, 85 percent; eliminating racial discrimination, 84 percent; wiping out poverty, 83 percent; raising living standards around the world, 80 percent; finding cures for disease, 76 percent; and giving a college education to all qualified, 75 percent." [2]

The Creeds of Business

Given a conception of the role of the corporation based on social harmony, business leaders clearly face a problem in justifying their continued autonomy and privilege in the face of evident public displeasure with their performance and apprehension over their power. If many people in society now share goals whose fulfillment they do not regard as identical—or even compatible—with the production of goods and services for profit by privately owned and managed institutions, what should be the appropriate response of business?

American businessmen have been divided in their response since at least the turn of the century. In an earlier analysis of the opinions of executives, *The American Business Creed,* the sociologist Francis Sutton and his co-authors, the economists Seymour Harris, Carl Kaysen and James Tobin, distinguished between the "classical" and the "managerial" creed.[3] The classical creed argues that the business role in society is fundamentally passive; the businessman is embedded in a network of contractual and marketplace obligations over which he has limited control. His pursuit of profit and his fulfillment of the desires of his shareholders are matters neither of greed nor of discretion, but an indication of how successfully he has served the social welfare.

The managerial creed, on the other hand, expands the boundaries of executive discretion, and hence managerial power and responsibility. Profits, or obligations to shareholders, are seen as a necessary but not sufficient measure of the boundaries of corporate responsibility; rather, the executive should consciously make decisions that balance the often competing, though legitimate, claims of shareholders, employees, customers, and the general public. An executive at Standard Oil of New Jersey articulated this conception of the objectives of the modern corporation over a decade ago:

> We like to feel that it is a good place for people to work. We have equal responsibilities to other groups: stockholders, customers, and the public generally, including government. What is the proper balance for the claims of these different sections? What part of profits should go to the stockholders? What part to the employees' wages? What part to the customer in lower prices and improved quality? Keeping the proper balance in these things is one of the most important matters that corporate management has to consider.[4]

A more recent (1974) formal statement of corporate objectives by another major oil company includes this section:

Relations with Stakeholders

1. [The company] will conduct its businesses and its relations with customers, other business entities, governments and the public at the highest level of ethics and integrity. [The company] will be a good citizen and an asset to each community in which it operates.

2. [The company] will serve its customers with products and services which meet their needs and desires, recognizing always that the enterprise cannot survive without customers.

3. [The company] will maintain a dividend policy consistent with long-range profit growth of the company with the objective that dividends, combined with the appreciation in market value of the company's common stock, will fairly compensate the shareholder for his investment.

4. [The company] will maintain relative levels of equity and debt which, when combined with the profit record, will demonstrate prudent management to the financial community and other investors.

5. [The company] will be an equal opportunity employer and will provide employees with a working environment in which they can achieve their potentials and be compensated in a manner commensurate with their performance.

The dichotomy between the "classical" and the "managerial" creeds thus continues to affect the response of the business community to challenges to its authority and power. But the split seems to exist less as one between one faction of business executives and another than as a conflict within the minds of individual businessmen.

A third ideological element has been emerging as well—a belief that business must reorient or at least modify its traditional commitment to private economic development by seeking to accommodate to the public's continually changing political and social expectations. Several businessmen at the conference argued that the privileges of business will depend on the extent to which corporations listen to, correctly interpret, and effectively respond to the political and social preferences of the American people:

> *The corporation is a creature of society. The public has given us a franchise and they have a perfect right to take it away. The Constitution didn't legitimate the corporation or the free enterprise system.*

> *The social responsibility of business is to create material abundance, but to do so on the basis of the ground rules that society sets.*

> *We are hired guns. It is simply a matter of someone pointing us in the right direction.*

This thread in business thinking we shall call "the doctrine of public consent," or, more briefly, "the consent creed." It represents an effort to base the legitimacy of the corporation on the principle of popular sovereignty; in effect, it seeks to apply to the corporation the legitimating concept of John Locke that a government rules only with the consent of the governed, the idea that animated the makers of the revolution whose bicentennial we are now celebrating. The "consent creed" of business would found the "just powers" of the corporation on democratic principles, just as the Declaration of Independence asserted that governments derive "their just powers from the consent of the governed." But the "consent creed" of business must be interpreted only analogically, not literally—for no American business executive really wants to hand over direct control of the corporation to the electorate; many businessmen simply want to assert their willingness to be responsive to public desires and rules and to base their claim to legitimacy and their right to exercise economic power on that willingness. They declare that they are prepared to be "accountable," but are not clear on what forms their "public accountability" should take or what social mechanisms should be used to insure it.

It is important not to exaggerate the sharpness of the ideological divisions within the business community. Only a relatively few executives articulate a perspective that could be classified unambiguously into one or the other category. Each of the three creeds here named—classical, managerial, and public consent—is best understood as an "ideal type," useful in demonstrating and clarifying the range and variety of contemporary business opinions. Most executives probably include elements of all three positions in their thinking. Among the senior executives represented at the 1974–75 conferences, the classical strain seemed dominant:

> *Our role is what it has always been: to meet material needs. That is our special area of competence. We are not responsible for establishing society's goals or values or for changing social behavior. By providing a right product in a right manner, business fulfills its responsibility for society.*
>
> *Corporations are special-purpose institutions.*

The owners of each business enterprise should define the social responsibility of their enterprise as they see fit. This is the only way compatible with the rights of their owners.

Many argued that the concept of "social responsibility," inherent in the consent creed, implies that the traditional business pursuit of profits and growth is not automatically in the best interests of society—a notion with which they strongly disagreed. One businessman suggested:

I can't believe that social responsibility was ever invented by a businessman; it must have been made up by a sociologist.

To be responsible to our workers, owners and customers is our routine function.

Business is not to be charged with responsibility for meeting spiritual or emotional needs. Business is to be charged for responsibility for meeting material needs.

Many of the same executives were willing to accept, in principle, the concept that the corporation has responsibilities to constituencies beyond its owners—the managerial creed. They contended, however, that the needs of these outside constituencies are best served if the corporation devotes its full energies to serving its shareholders. The successful maximization of profits is possible only if consumers receive a fair product at a fair cost; increased sales in turn enable the firm to employ more people and provide them and their families with a decent standard of living. Higher profits will mean more tax revenues. In short, the corporation will best fulfill its obligation to society by fulfilling its obligation to itself:

The corporation is ill-equipped to accept a major role in changing social policies.

The social responsibility of business is to make profits.

The business system is the patient, not the doctor.

Many corporate executives contended that if they try to operate outside their special area of competence, they will invariably get into trouble:

We shouldn't accept responsibility for what we don't know about.

Several businessmen expressed particular opposition to the concept of a social audit and conveyed to their fellow executives their thoroughly unpleasant and unproductive experiences with it. Either the social audit gives the auditors —usually drawn from outside groups or institutions whose attitudes toward the firm are held to be unsympathetic or worse—the opportunity to publicize those aspects of the firm's performance that offends them, or

It tends to make us congratulate ourselves for being heroes, for doing things any intelligent businessman will do anyway.

We tried the social audit. It wasn't worth a damn.

The social audit is a device for consulting firms to make money.

These executives are not necessarily opposed to the corporation's assuming social responsibility, but feel that their "nonbusiness" contributions should be voluntary. They are particularly concerned that the criteria for evaluating a firm's social contribution not deviate significantly from or detract from its economic performance. As one executive put it:

> *If you want to engage in programs of social improvement, don't do it in your role as a businessman.*

Government does have legitimate jobs to perform—which business supports. By paying taxes, the corporation more than adequately fulfills its social obligation:

> *We pay the government well. It should do its job and leave us alone to do ours.*

The Slow Transition

Many of the things one can hear American business executives saying today are echoes of what their forebears were saying nearly a century ago. A University of Michigan historian quotes Andrew Carnegie:

> The millionaires are the bees that make the most honey, and contribute most to the hive even after they have gorged themselves full. . . . Oh, these grand immutable, all-wise laws of natural forces, how perfectly they would work if human legislators would only let them alone! But no, they must be tinkering.

In the same source we read that the president of the New England Granite Works observed in the 1880's:

> [We are] overwhelmed . . . by useless legislation. The universal law of supply and demand is superior to any law which can be enacted by Congress or any other power on earth.[5]

By the turn of the century, however, these ideas and the social and political outlook they reflected had become irrelevant to the political, social, and economic structure of twentieth century American capitalism. The persuasiveness of this limited understanding of the role of business in society had derived from four assumptions: a competitive market, the identity of the firm with the private property of its owners, the limited participation of the government in the economy, and a belief in the separation of the economic and social spheres of society.

Each of these assumptions was gradually undermined by the close of the nineteenth century. Between 1895 and 1900, a merger wave created over five thousand trusts covering practically every line of productive activity and markedly altering the structure of industrial markets.

John Moody, a conservative Wall Street publisher who compiled the first definitive account of the scope of corporate concentration—to provide the public with the "truth about the trusts" to counter the charges of the "muckrakers"—identified seven "Great Industrial Trusts" that dominated the American economy: United States Steel, Amalgamated Copper, American Smelting and Refining, American Sugar Refining, Consolidated Tobacco, International Mercantile Marine, and Standard Oil. Some economic historians have argued that the classical structure of market competition, with no firm having any independent influence over pricing, and unlimited freedom of entry for competitors, has always been a figment of the imagination of economic textbook writers, and all that happened at the turn of the century was that national monopolies replaced regional ones. Nevertheless, it is clear that the merger movements and the growth of giant corporations in the late nineteenth and twentieth centuries drastically altered the structure of markets, resulting in far greater concentration of power.[6]

The restructuring of the economy removed a second prop of the classical creed: the idea that the privately owned corporation could draw upon property ownership rights to legitimate the power of corporate managers. While the separation of ownership and managerial control did not become a part of the conventional wisdom until 1932, when Adolf A. Berle, Jr., and Gardiner C. Means published their classic *The Modern Corporation and Private Property*, the creation of U.S. Steel in 1901 by the financier J. P. Morgan marked the beginning of a trend toward the replacement of owners by professional managers. This trend has continued unabated throughout the twentieth century; currently, less than one-third of the top executives of the Fortune 500 industrials exerts effective ownership control over the firms they direct. The modern corporation is still private property, in the sense that ownership rights to its resources adhere to individuals; but, as Berle and Means suggested in their pioneering 1932 study of the pattern of ownership of publicly held corporations:

> This dissolution of the atom of property (the separation of formal ownership and effective control) destroys the very foundation on which the economic order of the past three centuries has rested.[7]

The basic principle of "individual initiative in individual enterprise" had been challenged; the autonomy of management could no longer reasonably be defended on the basis that the firm was "their" private property.

The growth of the great corporations also brought in its train a much expanded role of government in the economy. Pressures from business interests concerned about insuring a greater degree of market stability and also from citizen and consumer interests concerned about the political dangers of unregulated monopoly forced the federal government, for the first time in American history, to systematically intervene in business affairs. By the time the Progressive Era had run its course, a variety of reforms and regulations covering rail transportation, food and drugs, trade, mergers and acquisitions, banking and much else had become accepted and integral parts of the American business setting.

Each of these developments, occurring concurrently over a short span of years, symbolized a broader transformation: the shift of the conception of the corporation from a private institution, whose impact was judged primarily in economic terms, to a quasi-public institution whose impact was seen in its social and political dimensions as well. It has been a century since social observers began to compare great modern corporations to nation-states. Shortly after the turn of the century, a contemporary observer wrote:

> U.S. Steel receives and expends more money every year than any but the very greatest of the world's national governments; its debt is larger than that of many of the lesser nations of Europe; it absolutely controls the destinies of a population nearly as large as that of Maryland and Nebraska, and indirectly influences twice that number.[8]

In his influential indictment of Standard Oil in *Wealth Against Commonwealth,* published in 1894, Henry Demarest Lloyd declared:

We have been fighting fire on the well-worn lines of old and leaving competition to regulate itself. But the flames of a new economic evolution run around us, and we turn to find that competition has killed competition, that corporations are grown greater than the State and have bred individuals greater than themselves, and that the naked issue of our time is with property becoming master instead of servant. . . .

Some business leaders responded to the charge that they had become the unelected rulers of "an extra-constitutional government" by reaffirming their faith in the discipline of the market and the sanctity of private property. Others recognized that the classical defense of enterprise had become inappropriate, and began to heed admonitions such as that offered by Arthur Twining Hadley, president of Yale University and an economist. In an essay entitled "Ethics and Corporate Management," written in 1906, Hadley suggested to the business community that:

Industrial corporations grew up into power because they met the needs of the past. To stay in power, they must meet the needs of the present, and arrange their ethics accordingly. . . . Those who fear the effects of increased government activity must prove by their acceptance of ethical duties to the public that they are not blind devotees of an industrial past which has ceased to exist, but are preparing to accept the heavier burdens and obligations which the industrial present carries with it.[10]

George Perkins of U.S. Steel responded two years later. His was one of the first formal statements from a member of the business community to acknowledge the social responsibility of business. He said:

> The larger the corporation becomes, the greater become its responsibilities to the entire community. The corporations of the future must be those that are semi-public servants, serving the public, with ownership widespread among the public, and with labor so fairly and equitably treated that it will look upon its corporation as its friend.

By 1914 Walter Lippmann could note in his epitaph to the Progressive Movement, *Drift and Mastery:*

> The cultural basis of property is radically altered, however much the law may lag behind in recognizing the change. . . . The men connected with these essential properties cannot escape the fact that they are expected to act increasingly like public officials. . . . What they will learn is that it is no longer their business. . . . Big businessmen who are all intelligent recognize this. They are talking more and more about their "responsibilities," their "stewardship." [11]

At the 1974–75 meetings held by The Conference Board, the "progressive" businessmen were still seeking to express this concept:

> *Social responsibility is nothing more than accepting a positive role in helping society achieve its goals.*
>
> *Who should define the social responsibility of business? The society as a whole. The corporation is a creature of society.*
>
> *The maximization of profits has to be maintained in a social, as well as an economic, context.*

General Electric, which has a half-century of history of particular sensitivity to and awareness of the sociopolitical environment of business, has made the consent doctrine a part of its official corporate policy. This was quoted by V. B. Day, Vice President, Industrial Relations, in a talk on "The Social Responsibility of Business" on December 3, 1969:

> The Corporation is a creature of society whose purpose is the production and distribution of needed goods and services, to the profit of society itself.

The Modern Consent Doctrine

While clearly derived from the doctrine of corporate social responsibility that dates from the turn of the century, these recent statements betray an important innovation. No longer is the corporation's "conscience" to be the sole judge of how management fulfills its obligations to society, but society itself has a right to define and shape corporate actions and objectives.

The problem that has always troubled critics and would-be reformers of the modern corporation is by what criteria executives should make judgments about what is in the best interests of the various constituencies of the corporation or of society. After all, they are not philosophers or political statesmen; nobody elected them to represent broad public interest; they got their high positions presumably because they knew how to produce certain goods or sell them, how to raise money or handle the company's legal problems, or to perform

that complex and ill-defined art "Management." They presumably have an above-average grasp of business decision-
making. But is there any particular reason why they should
be considered qualified to make judgments about "the best
interests" of the constituencies upon whom their organizations
have a major impact? What guarantee does society have that
a group of men formally elected by and legally responsible
to a group of largely anonymous shareholders (in fact, an
inner group of directors and other corporate officers) will,
upon assuming office, acquire a judicious sensitivity to the
common interest—a sensitivity that is not even particularly
noticeable among publicly elected officials? It is for this reason that, amid all the talk of the social responsibilities of
business, the notion that corporate officials derive their authority from society has remained, in Ben Seligman's term,
"otiose"—lazy, ineffective, of no use.[12]

In *The Twentieth Century Capitalist Revolution,* which
remains the most clearheaded and articulate defense of the
modern large business corporation in over a generation,
the late Adolf A. Berle concluded by gently acknowledging
the still tenuous relationship between "corporate capitalism
and 'the city of God' ":

> Corporate managements, like others, knowingly or unknow-
> ingly, are constrained to work within a frame of surrounding
> conceptions which in time impose themselves. The price of
> failure to understand and observe them is decay of the
> corporation itself. *Such conceptions emerge in time as law.*
> It may be said of the corporation as old Bracton said of the
> Crown: "There is no king where the will and not the law
> prevails." [Italics added.] [13]

As long as management was able, in the words of one executive, "to write its own ticket and define social responsibility," its usefulness as a rationalization and defense of business power was seriously limited. It is the emergence of countervailing political factions and institutionalized laws and controls that has made the portrait of executives "balancing" their own interests and the competing interests of shareholders, consumers, workers, local communities and government agencies at various levels a more reasonable description of reality.

In a real sense, the political mobilization achieved by the environmental, consumer, and antiwar movements, the pressures of trade unions, and, most importantly, the power of government, has served to reinforce the principle that the corporation's power is based on public consent.

Today corporate executives must consider nonshareholder constituencies in making decisions. For executives to argue, then, that it is "society that defines the social responsibility of business," is no longer lazy rhetoric: it is a frank acknowledgment of the legal and political constraints that have been placed upon business. The corporation's acceptance of the legitimacy of the public's participation in shaping the scope of business policy is reflected in statements by business executives. In 1973, John Connor, Chairman of the Board of Allied Chemical and a former Secretary of Commerce, told the 15th Annual Business Conference at Rutgers University:

> If [we] are to survive the crunch of the years ahead . . . we businessmen must enlarge our traditional concept of what that role is and what it should be. We need to perform con-

vincingly in carrying out all the many social responsibilities identified by and for business in recent years, from environmental control to providing jobs for minorities where more needs to be done. . . . In short, we will have to be more responsive to public pressures.

At the 1974–75 Conferences we heard:

The public defines social responsibility in their roles as consumers and citizens. We have to respect public preferences.

As businessmen we will not set the goals of business. Unfortunately, the government will be the most influential. Government created the corporation and can insist on controlling it.

Unless our private enterprise structure enables our society to achieve its goals, it will be replaced. We, therefore, in business are required to make the [political] process succeed even when we disapprove of the goals that have been established. Business is only one of the elements involved in input for the goal-setting process which is essentially political in nature.

It is the political process and decisions which will ultimately determine the success or failure of our private enterprise system.

State Mercantilism

The doctrine of "public consent" bears a certain relationship to the so-called "state mercantilism" that characterized the first half-century of the American republic. Although forgotten by all but a few scholars, the most important economic factor in the United States up until the Civil War were the state governments. Through extensive subsidies, the backing of loans, the granting of exclusive privileges, the establishing of business-government partnerships and other acts of assistance to business, state and local governments played a pioneering role in establishing the infrastructure that made the subsequent industrialization of the United States possible.

The major vehicle through which both private and public resources were devoted to economic development was the state-chartered corporation. It was through the chartering device that community needs and private energies were brought together. Corporations were chartered for specific public purpose, especially to construct much needed transportation facilities. They had government-appointed representatives on their boards of directors, were allowed to operate only in specified geographic areas, and could remain in existence only for finite periods of time. The provisions of each corporate charter were specifically approved by the state legislatures, and the privileges the charters granted could be revoked periodically by the appropriate government authorities. The corporation was, in the first instance, a contract between private individuals and the state; the state defended the privileges and defined duties of corporations, and the early nineteenth-century business corporation did, in fact, owe its existence to the popular franchise. Historian Robert A. Lively summarizes the situation:

> . . . the public official [rather than] the individual enterpriser [was] the key figure in the release of capitalist energy, the public treasury rather than private saving [was] the major

source of venture capital, and community purpose out-
weighed personal ambition in the selection of large goals for
local economies.[14]

Beginning in 1837, when the first General Incorporation
Act was passed by the state of Connecticut, the restrictions
placed on managerial autonomy by the government were
gradually lifted, and continuing through the next five decades,
management enjoyed an extraordinary degree of protection
from legal interference from the public, whether acting in
their capacities as citizens or as stockholders. This was the
heyday of the classical free enterprise corporate ideology, and
of its extreme form, social Darwinism.

The Power of Government

The intimate relationship between the state and business
that characterized the business corporations chartered by the
British Crown to engage in overseas exploration and trade—
from which model the American states derived their institutions—was relatively unambiguous: the Crown was clearly
on top. To cite this historical analogy is also to reveal one of
its important limitations as a model for business-government
relations that few businessmen today would accept.

While the balance of power between the entrepreneurs and
the American states was not quite as skewed in the early years
of the Republic, there was little question in the minds of most
citizens that the states had the ultimate authority, including
the power of life and death over the corporation. Although
there were frequent outbursts of resentment against the privileges of particular corporations—Jackson's struggle against

the chartering of the Bank of the United States is the most memorable—there is little question that during the nation's first half-century, the locus of power and prestige rested with the state, not the corporation. At the same time, the wide degree of public support for rapid economic development made the issue of political control and private gain manageable. A contemporary comparison might be with the relationship between a company holding a sports franchise and a local community. That the financial rewards of a championship season go almost exclusively and disproportionately to the team's owners and players is likely to be overlooked by the community's fans, proud of having "their" local team triumph—and hopeful of the indirect benefits to the community's economy from tourism, hotel and restaurant business, the attraction or retention of corporate headquarters, jobs, etc. There were presumably reasons why a financially hard-pressed New York City would invest over fifty million dollars in rebuilding Yankee Stadium for the Yankees' management. But if the team fails, the compatibility between public and private interest may break apart.

Whatever may have been the case in the early nineteenth century, few outside the business community believe any more in the automatic and universal compatibility of business and public objectives. We are a society whose members hold a wide diversity of opinions about national goals and priorities. It would be reasonable to expect frequent conflicts between the preferences of business executives and elected government officials if they were yoked together. Accordingly, the issue of the political power of government *versus* business becomes critical. While the classical creed justifies the autonomy of business by emphasizing its efficiency, its independence and distance from government, and its subservience to the market, the doctrine of public consent requires a government that is regarded as fair, responsive to citizen needs and pressures, and as a reliable conduit between "society" and business. But public faith in government has declined, together with public faith in business. And if business were capable of imposing its own public-policy preferences upon the nation, despite the efforts of the majority of citizens to control the political process, then the "consent" doctrine might become worse than "otiose": it would become a euphemism for "state capitalism" or "fascism."

Public acceptance of the legitimacy of the role of the business corporation comes to an important extent to rest on the responsiveness and openness of the government. It is the democratic political process that gives the corporation the "right" to exercise power and at the same time assures that such power will be wielded or controlled in accordance with the preferences of the public.

The crucial issue is how to redefine the interdependency of business and government in the American setting. While there has always been a connection between the justification for these two vital institutions—the terms "democracy" and "freedom" have signified both political democracy and entrepreneurial freedom throughout American history—the erosion of the classical liberal distinction between "public" and "private" spheres of society has exacerbated the tension between the two institutions. The scope and safeguarding of privacy in the area of personal life has recently been expanded, but the privacy of economic activity finds itself increasingly undermined and limited.

We have always known that economic activity has a public

dimension, but the worry of businessmen today is that it may no longer have a private dimension. Corporate decisions affect the relative prosperity of various regions of our nation, the development of foreign nations, submission or resistance to foreign boycott threats, discrimination or nondiscrimination against blacks, women, Jews, or other social groups, the future of cities, the quality of urban life, the retirement income of the aged, the development and conservation of energy, the state of the environment, and even the viability of human life itself. There is virtually nothing a corporation does any more that can be considered exclusively "its own business."

Few Americans now believe that the corporations can be trusted to perform their functions satisfactorily in the absence of regulations that limit the discretion of executives and circumscribe the dictates of the market. On few issues is there such wide public consensus as on the importance and necessity of government regulation of business, if business is to serve the community's interests. The Harris poll reports that over 80 percent of the American people believe that, "if left alone, big business would be greedy, selfish, make inordinate profits at the expense of the public," and that, "if left unchecked, big business would stifle competition." [15] Public confidence in the leadership of business has apparently been gravely weakened by revelations of corporate attempts to unduly influence government policy.

The business community thus finds itself in an awkward dilemma. On one side, executives are in virtually unanimous agreement that business must more forcefully present its point of view to the government officials whose decisions play such a decisive role in shaping their corporate welfare, and must participate more actively in the formation of public policy; on the other side, they are fearful that as they do, public opposition to their political role will intensify, together with public measures to hamstring the corporations. Nevertheless, most businessmen seem determined to bring their influence to bear upon government. Two comments by Irving S. Shapiro, chairman of E. I. du Pont, are relevant:

> We find ourselves in an adversary relationship with the bureaucracy. We must find a way of making government a partner with business.
>
> Too often business and government confront each other as adversaries—a relationship which is a throwback to an earlier day. The nation can no longer afford this.[16]

Other typical statements on the theme were made at the conferences:

> *If we abdicate our responsibility to take positions on political issues, the profit we produce will be turned against us. We must get involved in the making of laws more than ever before.*
>
> *We must seek out ways to achieve really fruitful cooperation between business and government and eliminate the adversary relationship between them, based as it is on the assumption that the public needs protection from the world of big business.*

What is "responsible" public policy or business-government cooperation from a corporate perspective, however, is often a "governmental handout to business," or a sellout, from the viewpoint of the public. Most businessmen assert that they do not equate "effective political participation" with undue influence. They are critical of those firms that heeded the admonitions of Mr. Nixon's fund-raisers in order to protect themselves from the "fanatics" at the Environmental Protection Agency, or to get a new air-traffic route, or to safeguard a television channel, or to fend off the closing of a tax loophole, and subsequently found both themselves—and their companies—the target of public scorn and attack that may take years to wear off and may cause immeasurable damage to their institutions—and to public respect for government as well. A corporation known by the "politicians it keeps" may for a time provide its executives with a feeling of security, but sooner or later it undermines the public's confidence (and business's own confidence) in the one institution charged with representing the interest of all—the government. Executives, who themselves are the source of no small share of the public abuse routinely directed against government, are insufficiently sensitive to the links between public confidence in government and public confidence in business; in effect, they are "the establishment," or at least its two principal pillars. A few businessmen at the conferences recognized this. Said one:

> *We must enhance the credibility of our political institutions. The public thinks we are in an unholy alliance with the regulatory agencies. They think that business and government are in bed together.*

The Consent Creed and Political Action

As a business ideology, the doctrine of public consent is, as we have noted, a variant of the original liberal philosophy upon which a group of farmers and merchants based their revolution against their legal government two hundred years ago. That philosophy, associated most closely with the names of John Locke in England, Jean Jacques Rousseau in France, and Thomas Jefferson in America, held that government rests upon the consent of the governed—and that, whenever any form of government became destructive to the ends for which it was established, to secure certain human rights, among them life, liberty and the pursuit of happiness, the people have the right to abolish it, and institute a new government.

The corporate "consent creed" is neither so clear nor so dramatic. It argues, somewhat metaphorically, that the corporation derives its franchise from public consent, and if the public is dissatisfied with its performance, it has, as one businessman said, "a perfect right to take it away." But there is an important difference in the consent creed from the social contract of Locke, Rousseau, and Jefferson—and one that may spare corporations from the fate that overtook the government of George III in the American colonies. For, unlike the Lockean "social contract," the "contract" between the corporation and society is subject to mutual negotiation; it bears a closer resemblance to a normal business contract. By contrast, for the seventeenth- and eighteenth-century liberal philosophers, the government played no part in setting the terms of the social contract its citizens made with it; its right to defend itself from the withdrawal of consent by its citizens was acknowledged only implicitly. Accordingly, while the corporate "social contract" acknowledges the public's right to impose its preferences upon business, it also acknowledges the corporation's participation in shaping those preferences in accordance with management's judgment of its own and society's best interests.

If, as the classical business ideology maintained, the only legitimate mechanism through which the public could shape the policies of business was the marketplace, then business's own attempts to shape the public's desires should be confined to influencing product preferences; the corporation's role in creating social values, to be consistent, should be a passive one. It should "stay out of politics" or at least not use government to further its own economic ends—or its preferences for social ends. But if, on the other hand, businessmen acknowledge that the public has the right to seek to influence, guide, or control the corporation through the political process, as well as in the marketplace, then business may appropriately play an active role in influencing the political values and choices of the community.

The consent doctrine thus mandates a politically active role for business. Business has every right to participate more actively in the process of setting economic and social goals for the country, as long as it does so honestly and openly.

Our life is closely interwoven with politics. We should maximize our efforts to set social goals. Democracy is a rough game and we have got to learn how to play it.

As the arena of decision-making shifts from the marketplace to government, and as the content of the demands raised on business becomes more complex, the struggle for "the hearts and minds," and not simply the brand loyalties, of the public becomes critical for the corporation. It is the issue of redefining the social contract between business and society that has become the central concern of the current leaders of American business.

CHAPTER SIX

Corporate Autonomy
and Political Freedom

EVERY BUSINESS EXECUTIVE regards an adequate level of profits as the *sine qua non* of corporate autonomy—and sees the lure of higher profits as the driving force behind a more effective economic performance.

Even those businessmen who accept the importance of gaining public consent for the way they run their corporations stress the necessity of good profits. But some add that profits are not, or should not be, the sole purpose of business enterprise. Thus, Fletcher Byrom, chairman of the Koppers Corporation, said in a 1974 speech:

> Profits are to a corporation what breathing is to human life. We cannot live without breathing, and a corporation cannot live in a private enterprise system without profits. But breathing is not the sole purpose of life, and profits are not the sole purpose of the adventure that we call business management.

Frederick R. Kappel, then chairman of AT&T, said essentially the same thing in 1964:

> When someone asked me, which do you put first in your mind, service or profits, I said naturally I put service first, but we can only serve by earning money.[1]

There have been many expressions by corporate executives of their willingness to respond to new social demands:

> *Business must adjust to its new partners and accept them on the basis of equality.*

> *We have got to be more flexible in our attitude toward public-interest groups and more responsive to the concern about the quality of life.*

And in a commencement address at Oklahoma Christian College in August 1974, M. A. Wright, Chairman and Chief Executive of Exxon Co., USA, said:

> Whatever its faults, free enterprise is responsive; it operates only with public consent. And in continually adjusting to the public will, free enterprise is the nation's number one problem solver. Industry's impressive achievements in the area of environmental protection are an outstanding example of the constructive response of free enterprise to community demands.

But the executives continually stressed the importance of keeping social demands "within reason," that is, with sufficient scope for private profit and without excessive transfer of resources from the private to the public sector.

The Tension between Public and Private Sectors

Virtually every public issue affecting the corporation that has surfaced over the last decade—including consumer and environmental protection, occupational health and safety, disclosure, corporate intervention in the political process, the morality of corporate investment decisions, the equity and incentives or disincentives of taxation, the morale and participation of employees, job opportunities for women and minorities, the role of banking and business in the inner cities—reflects the fundamental tension between the imperatives of private accumulation of profit and economic efficiency on one side and social expectations or demands on the other. Businessmen insist that a fair balance must be struck:

> *Business should be regulated, but it must be within the framework of our business system and its ability to achieve its goals.*

> *Clean air, equal opportunity, and a sound environment— these are part of the public's expectation of business and we should take them seriously. The public first needs to understand their costs.*

And they maintain that what is at stake is not just their private interests but the survival of an economic system on which political freedom depends.

> *The issue is not corporate involvement in social change, but preserving our autonomy.*

The main social responsibility of business is to insure the survival of the free enterprise system.

But the critics of such arguments maintain that corporate executives are struggling to maintain a myth—the myth that the great corporations are private enterprises. Thus the political scientist Robert Dahl writes:

> Whatever may be the optimal way of governing the great corporations, surely it is a delusion to consider it a *private* enterprise. General Motors is as much a public enterprise as the U.S. Post Office . . . wholly dependent for its survival during every second of its operations on a vast network of laws, protection, services, inducement, constraints, and coercions provided by innumerable governments. . . . GM is *de facto* the public's business. . . . It would be more realistic to think of all economic enterprise as a public service.[2]

At the 1974–75 conferences, a number of executives recognized that they were indeed doing "the public's business":

> *We can see that corporations are often legally placed in positions of carrying out government policy. We decide to clean up the air and water, and by law corporations must implement anti-pollution programs. The nation decides to legislate codes of conduct in employment practices, and it is the company nondiscrimination program which makes policy reality. The government sets safety standards for assorted products, and the private-sector mechanism develops the designs and materials which meet those standards. The national monetary policy is established by our central bank, but member banks carry it out. The concept*

*of a corporation as an instrument of public policy or
international affairs is becoming more important and
accepted.*

But the political conservatives fear that there is a serious
danger that acceptance of such a concept of public responsibility by the corporations will end in state control of business.
Friederich Hayek, the self-styled "Whig" writes:

> So long as the management is supposed to serve the interest
> of the stockholders, it is reasonable to leave the control of
> its action to the stockholders. But if the management is sup-
> posed to serve wider public interests, it becomes merely a
> logical consequence of this conception that the appointed
> representatives of the public interest should control the
> management.[3]

And Henry Manne, Professor of Law and Political Science at
the University of Rochester, concludes:

> Every time businessmen acknowledge a public interest in
> what they do, they invite political control of their activities.
> They should be more careful of the company they keep.[4]

Businessmen, with rare exceptions, fear the loss of efficiency that they believe would inevitably follow from greater
political control. "Do we want the entire economy run like the
Post Office?" is a common question. The current economic
and political troubles of the Tennessee Valley Authority are
viewed with glum satisfaction by many businessmen—confir-
mation of their faith in the inability of an economic institution to operate efficiently without the discipline and incentives of the profit motive:

Corporations can plan; government can't.

Government is the most ineffective allocator of them all.

The private sector is more innovative because its god is profits. In government there is no driving force.

Every function the private sector does, the government could do. The difference is that the private sector can take risks and make mistakes. The government is a very conservative producer.

While most American businessmen still believe what they are saying about the inherent superiority of private enterprise over government management, they have become aware of the superior growth performance of a number of foreign economies in which government plays a large role, in many cases larger than does the United States government. Between 1960 and 1970—a decade of virtually uninterrupted growth in the United States—this country's economic growth rate ranked eighteenth out of the twenty most advanced democratic, industrial countries. Although part of this more rapid growth in other industrial countries was attributable to new plant and technology made possible by American aid, it is still clear that at existing exchange rates the gap in per capita income between the United States and Switzerland, Sweden, West Germany and France was virtually closed.

Some conservatives attribute this record to better economic policies of some foreign governments—policies more sensitive to the needs of the private business sector. The editorial page editor of *The Wall Street Journal* wrote a column in 1975 praising the care taken by the social democratic government of Sweden (once anathema to American businessmen) to ensure that business profits, investments and foreign competitiveness are safeguarded.[5] Many corporate executives, far less insulated and more cosmopolitan than at any other time, thanks to their multinational and transnational roles, now regard with greater comprehension and even cautious sympathy government-business relations in such countries as Japan and France, where the state is in closer partnership with business and plays a more sustaining and guiding role in the economy and foreign trade.[6] Détente with the Soviet Union and mainland China has even led many American businessmen to look at the Communist states with greater pragmatism and less hysteria. And many are aware of the critical role played by government in the oil-producing and other developing countries.

Even if some American business leaders no longer believe in the universal applicability or inherent superiority of the American system, nevertheless very few, if any, wish to import foreign designs. There was not a single reference in any of the conferences to another nation as providing a model for the United States:

> I cannot think of any example of a government-business relationship in the world that is working well and that we should try to emulate.

The reason, commonly expressed, is the threat to political freedom:

> It can be argued that the economy is not harmed at all by the growth in transfer payments—to almost any level. After all, the money is spent, goods and services are produced and employment is maintained in doing so. But that's not the

point. In socialist countries goods and services are produced and employment is maintained, but the difference is one of freedom. Should the worker-producer have and control most of the income realized from his labor or should he hand it over to the control of government to redistribute it in turn, to others to spend?

The Economics of Freedom

Although the economic systems of Japan, China, Iran, Kuwait, and France may be most appropriate for their citizens, business executives believe they do not merit our emulation, because they have purchased their economic accomplishments at the cost of freedom. The virtue of the American system, they assert, does not rest solely on its economic accomplishments, but on its unique ability to combine these accomplishments with economic and political liberty.

If we can only manage to stay alive, we will make a contribution to the preservation of some semblance of a free market, competition, economic freedom and a free society.

It is not coincidence that we speak of free speech in terms of "the marketplace of ideas." Political and economic freedom are closely related.

There aren't any social goals that businessmen as a group or class are likely to agree on other than promotion of economic freedom.

In Treasury Secretary William Simon's words, "If you lose your economic freedom, I can guarantee you that you will lose your personal freedom as well." [7]

The original Lockean justification for private property was that a wide distribution of economic rights would promote a decentralization of political power. Economic freedom was valuable not for its own sake, but because it resulted in the preservation of political liberty—and this is an argument that American businessmen still strongly believe and affirm. However, despite assertions by business executives that political and economic freedom are indivisible, or even identical, it was clear that, in the minds of the numerous conference participants who expressed themselves on the issue, the most relevant meaning of freedom is economic.

One of the reasons for this apparent discrepancy may be the highly specialized education and experience of business executives and a corresponding, if lesser, specialization among government administrators and congressmen and their staffs. With the separation of ownership and management, business management became a profession for which many of the younger top executives deliberately trained. At the same time, as government—particularly the federal government—became involved in more and more technical issues, the individuals dealing with them also developed the narrow outlook of specialists. On the one hand, this trend may be an added factor in public-private sector tensions by narrowing the parties' perspectives. On the other, however, the mutual interests of specialists may provide a basis for discussion and the resolution of problems. One can find many instances to illustrate both these associative and dissociative tendencies among business executives and public officials.

Businessmen consider themselves free to the extent that they have significant control over the forces that shape their economic choices and are able to make decisions about how to use the resources entrusted to them; they believe that they should personally reap a share of the rewards—or suffer the consequences. Businessmen and bankers appear to defend freedom and civil liberties primarily when their economic interests are directly affected—as by government inspection of the foreign transfers of banks. Many businesses, on the other hand, have submitted to demands by foreign states that they discriminate against fellow American citizens, as in the case of the Arab boycott of Jewish firms, as a condition of doing business.

If economic and political freedom were automatically and necessarily interdependent, the participants at these conferences would certainly be among the freest individuals in American society: their wealth, income, and high managerial status would appear to give them a degree of independence beyond that of the great majority of their fellow citizens. One might expect American businessmen to feel free to express their views openly and strongly on any social or political subject. The reality is quite different. American businessmen are extremely cautious and wary in how they use their freedom or express their views in public. Save for a few exceptions or eccentrics, American businessmen are conspicuous for their inconspicuousness. The reason for this may be, in fact, their "managerial ideology" that came with the awareness that they must mediate among the interests and preferences of a wide range of constituencies, and they can best do this by being as bland and generally acceptable as possible lest they give offense and the corporation get into trouble. William H. Whyte's penetrating portrait of "the organization man" as conformist remains as fresh today as when it was written twenty years ago.[8] By the time corporate managers reach the top, for their relatively brief tenure, their independence of spirit or mind seems, characteristically, to have been attenuated by the organization. They seem less able than those not habituated to organizational life to stand up to strong external pressures. This may help to explain why corporate executives were so compliant in making illegal political contributions when a President's fund-raisers brought pressure upon them to do so.

Only a few business executives stood up to the implicit blackmail (or promise of favors to come) held out by the fund-raisers of the Committee to Reelect the President. Bob Dorsey, Chairman of the Board of Gulf Oil, said: "We felt the pressure to be irresistible." And George Spater, chairman of American Airlines, told a Senate Committee:

> It is something like the old Medieval maps that show a flat world and then what they call *terra incognita* with fierce animals lying around the fringes of this map. You just don't know what is going to happen to you if you get off it.

Indeed, there is a temptation to suggest (at least half-seriously) that Watergate demonstrates that property ownership and the power to be free have become negatively correlated. As the London *Economist* observed on November 22, 1975:

> In these mid-1970s it is gradually becoming clear that ownership of the means of production is no longer a source of political or economic power, and may indeed now be a source of political and economic powerlessness. As the

realization of this sinks in, it is likely to turn a lot of present business planning—and of ageless political demagoguery —on its head. The first major consequence may be the beginning of the end of the age of very big multinational corporations.

The most obvious recent product of what yesterday's men now call the wicked meso-economic power of the multinational corporations is that American companies have for a decade been vilified for having kept open a proportion of Europe's (and particularly Britain's) car-making industry as what has increasingly looked like an act of charity. Now that Chrysler at last needs to shut a British operation on which it has been losing millions, this is called "putting a pistol to the prime minister's head." If a company that merely sold foreign-made cars to Britain, like Datsun, wanted to stop loss-making operations by ceasing to sell unprofitable lines, the secretary for trade would recommend its president for a knighthood. The makers of Datsun suffer political disabilities against taking sensible decisions only in the country where they own the means of production, because back home in Japan it is politically impossible for them to get out of loss-making by sacking all the workers they wish.

The realization of this will over the next few years seep through to big corporations' boardrooms.

A Time for Taking Stock

As we consider the state of our economy and polity for our third century, we ought to reexamine the relationship between political and economic freedom with open minds. While there undoubtedly remains an important legacy of truth in the classic Lockean theory that private ownership of property encourages widespread dispersion of political power and

therefore serves individual freedom, there is no clear relationship between the degree of government control of the economy and political liberty. One might well argue that placing
certain restrictions on enterpreneurial liberty, such as protecting the rights of workers to organize unions "of their own
choosing" or providing for greater economic security for the
less successful members of society, has actually enhanced
freedom in the democratic, capitalist nations, and that such
reforms (or controls) are, paradoxically, an integral part of
any advanced society that calls itself "free."

For the economic conditions of freedom have changed
radically since this nation was founded. Thomas Jefferson
thought that the way to ensure that the United States would
remain a nation of free men was to keep the economy essentially agrarian. Freedom, he thought, would flourish amid the
beauty of the countryside, on the open plains, in the vast river
valleys. He feared the contaminating effects of building an
urban and industrial society. "The mobs of great cities," said
Jefferson, "are like sores on the human body." If Americans
are "piled upon one another in large cities, as in Europe," he
said, "they shall become corrupt, as in Europe."

This notion that individual freedom could flourish only in
the country and the wilderness was widely held in Jefferson's
day—and not only in America. The English poet William
Blake asked:

> Why should I care for the men of Thames
> And the cheating waters of chartered streams
> Or shrink at the little blasts of fear
> That the hireling blows into mine ear?

> Though born on the cheating banks of Thames—
> Though his waters bathed my infant limbs—
> The Ohio shall wash his stains from me;
> I was born a slave, but I go to be free.

Today it might be pretty risky to bathe infant limbs in the Ohio. The factories along the Ohio add their share to the American problem of water pollution and air pollution. And up and down the land one finds cities that dwarf the European cities of Jefferson's day; but perhaps he was right in saying that the American cities would become as "corrupt."

When the United States was founded, more than four-fifths of the working people were independent farmers, and most of the rest were independent tradesmen or handicraftsmen. Today more than four-fifths of the labor force are paid employees; less than 7 percent are employed in agriculture and fewer still are what might be called "independent farmers." If Jefferson had been right in supposing that there was a vital link between individual freedom and an individualistic agrarian economy, then freedom would have long since vanished from this country. If it has not, it must be because the crucial link is not between freedom and agriculture, or even between freedom and a nation's legal and political institutions.

It is true that the authors of the United States Constitution looked upon private property as absolutely fundamental to individual freedom. (The foes of capitalism later looked upon private property exactly the other way around; the communists said they would liberate the workers from their capitalist oppressors by abolishing the capitalists' private property.) At the Constitutional Convention of 1787, the founding fathers saw private property as not so much one right, to be secured like other rights of citizenship, but rather, as the early nineteenth-century historian Richard Hildreth put it, as "the great and chief right, of more importance than all others." That may have been an overstatement, but the fifth amendment to the Constitution did declare that no person "shall be deprived of life, liberty, or property without due process of law," and it clearly considered property to be a vital element in safeguarding the individual against the state—or "the mob."

Private property was seen as the necessary material underpinning of the other precious freedoms of the individual—his freedom of speech, of religion, of assembly, and of voluntary association with his friends. To the authors of the Constitution, liberty did not mean merely majority rule, but, more fundamentally, it meant minority rights—individual rights— even when the individual was in a minority of one. For, if a man knew that he was secure in his property and could not be deprived of his means of livelihood as long as he broke no law, then he could stand up to any man and to any officer of government. (Of course, this assumed that government itself would act within the law.) Individual freedom can survive only if the individual has alternative private means of gaining a livelihood even if he incurs the disfavor or wrath of the state—that is, of the bureaucracy or politicians who control the state. If one sympathizes with Blake in disliking "the little blasts of fear that the hireling blows into mine ear," how much more one should loathe the mighty blasts of fear that the dictatorship of a monolithic state can blow.

Property rights are thus important to safeguard the freedom

even of individuals who own little property themselves; for a man's ability to change his job if he incurs the displeasure of his employer (or if the employer incurs *his* displeasure) is essential to the individual's independence and integrity.

In stressing the economic aspects of freedom, businessmen are by no means unique among Americans, for whom the prime meaning of freedom has long been freedom of opportunity, freedom to get ahead in the world. It was Henry Clay who, in a speech in the Senate in 1832, coined the phrase, "the self-made man." In 1897, Chauncey M. Depew declared upon the unveiling of a statue of Cornelius Vanderbilt:

> The American Commonwealth is built upon the individual. It recognizes neither classes nor masses. We have thus become a nation of self-made men. . . . Freedom of opportunity and preservation of the results of foresight, industry, thrift, and honesty have made the United States the most prosperous and wealthy nation in the world.

And it is revealing that, in 1975, four out of ten Americans base their description of the U. S. economic system on "the personal freedoms and opportunities for economic mobility inherent in the system for everyone—for the workers as well as entrepreneurs." When asked what is particularly good about the U. S. economic system, 39 percent emphasized individual mobility and economic opportunity. Only 20 percent mentioned specifically personal or political freedoms, while an additional 15 percent mentioned "freedom of choice." On the other hand, "both the communist and socialist systems, when measured against the American system," are perceived to have no individual freedom (62 percent and 44 percent, respectively) and no opportunities for betterment (24 percent and 16 percent). And, at the 1974–75 conferences, various business executives said:

> *Business can supply an opportunity to work. This means an opportunity to be poor if you don't work and an opportunity to be rich if you do.*

> *Business has the responsibility to provide the opportunity to achieve aspirations.*

> *Every time people have a choice—how to live, what to buy, where to work—they are getting the benefits of a free system.*

> *We owe all good things in America to the free market.*

But businessmen love free markets more in the abstract than in the concrete. Adam Smith, patron saint of free marketers, was under no illusion on that score; he observed that businessmen in the same trade "seldom meet together, whether for merriment and diversion, but the conversation ends up in a conspiracy against the public, or in some contrivance to raise prices." And, knowing the proclivity of businessmen to run to government for protection against competition, he warned that "the proposal of any new law for regulation of commerce which comes from this order of merchants and manufacturers ought always to be listened to with great precaution, and ought never to be adopted till having been long and carefully examined . . . with the most suspicious attention. It comes from an order of men, whose interest is never exactly the same with that of the public. . . ." A long list of subsequent acts of legislation or administration favored by businessmen in this country—"fair trade," oil-import quotas, "voluntary" restraints by foreign textile exporters, special tariff rules on certain imported chemicals, export subsidies, bans on the use of foreign vessels in American coastal shipping, etc.—suggests that not all that much has changed since Smith's day, although the internationalization of American business has given many corporations a strong interest in liberal international trade and investment rules.

On the domestic side, the antitrust laws are regarded by many executives of large corporations not as a means of safeguarding the "free market" but as an interference with "freedom of enterprise," that is, corporate autonomy. But, however vilified the Antitrust Division of the Justice Department or the Federal Trade Commission may be when they move to apply the antitrust laws in specific cases, antitrust is treated by many businessmen as a sacred cow, which it would be political folly to try to butcher.[10] Some businessmen occasionally praise antitrust in the abstract as an integral part of the American political and legal heritage; and of course the antitrust laws are sometimes a useful weapon against business competitors, especially the small against the big. Whether the antitrust laws have anything to do with it or not, competitiveness and the struggle for a larger share of the market remain very much a part of the American scene. The dynamism and aggressiveness of American companies toward each other greatly complicates the problem of how "business" as an entity should respond to widespread public criticism and hostility.

Is There a Business Community?

American businessmen today see themselves as a beleaguered group, locked in fierce political conflict with other
groups in the society and ultimately dependent on their own
resources for survival. As one executive put it:

> *No one really gives a damn about us—the government, the*
> *consumers, our workers.*

Only a rare business executive seems sympathetic or understanding of this social resentment. One executive said:

> *The average American wants to do the best he can for his*
> *family. We have pushed him. We have encouraged our*
> *customers to want the good life. Yet to do that they need*
> *more money. Why should we make so much more than they?*

While their critics talk of the shortcomings of "business"
or the "business community," for executives the dominant
reality is that business is usually a community in name only:
firms pursue their individual or industry's economic objectives, indifferent to the impact of their actions upon business
as a whole. But, when the public's attitude to business turns
critical, the relationship between the actions of individual
firms and the business system becomes dramatically transformed. When business as a whole—its performance, its
power, its legitimacy—is put on trial, each enterprise finds
itself in the dock, regardless of the extent to which it or even
its industry has been the target of public criticism. And it is

extremely difficult for the "business community" to respond because:

> *We don't have a business community. Just a fragmented*
> *bunch of self-interested people. When a particular industry*
> *is in trouble, like utilities or oil, it fights alone and everyone*
> *else turns their back. We haven't got a chance against*
> *George Meany as he speaks with one voice.*
>
> *We do have to get together, but it is hard as we don't*
> *agree.*

Businessmen themselves often complain of their "tunnel vision." They tell each other:

> *We have got to stop being so selfish and just care about*
> *meeting a payroll. We have to look out for the welfare of*
> *the free enterprise system.*

The American business community may be unusually amorphous in part because, unlike its counterparts in most other capitalist nations, it did not have to engage in a political and military struggle to break down barriers to the development of a market economy. Unlike the French or British bourgeoisie, which had to organize to overthrow a restrictive and repressive feudal system, American businessmen faced no such obstacle; from the beginning American business confronted a climate extraordinarily sympathetic to individual enterprise. Ironically, it is precisely the extent to which business has historically been unchallenged in America, either by an aristocracy or by a socialist working-class movement, that has kept American business from developing a clear sense of itself as a class, with a set of values, goals, and expectations distinct from those of the rest of the society.

The sense of classlessness that pervades American society, cited so frequently by both defenders and critics of America's unique political tradition, has also made American unions relatively indifferent to socialist ideology. As a leading historian of American labor, Selig Perlman, put it, American labor has been "job conscious," not "class conscious." [11]

The lack of a business leadership in the United States is the price American business pays for its extraordinary freedom from the kind of class conflict that has pervaded European capitalism. A century and a half ago, Tocqueville remarked,

> To tell the truth, though there are rich men, the class of rich men does not exist; for these individuals have no feelings or purposes, no traditions or hopes, in common; there are individuals, therefore, but no definite class. . . . The rich are not compactly united among themselves. . . .
>
> In their intense and exclusive anxiety to make a fortune, they lose sight of the close connection which exists between the private fortune of each of them and the prosperity of all. . . . The discharge of political duties appears to them to be a troublesome annoyance, which diverts them from their occupations and business. . . . These people think they are following the principle of self-interest, but the idea they entertain of that principle is a very rude one; and the better to look after what they call their business, they neglect their chief business, which is to remain their own masters.[12]

And his observation is still largely true. In some respects, the American business community today may be even more fragmented than in the past. At the height of his power, J. P. Morgan dominated the American business community and possessed the authority to speak for it. The most delicate negotiations regarding the boundaries of government intervention in the economy could be resolved by private conversations between President Theodore Roosevelt and J. P. Morgan. In effect, Morgan himself was the head of the banking system; the Federal Reserve Board did not exist.

While governmental authority has become considerably more centralized since 1900, the distribution of power within the business community has grown more widely distributed. The enormous size and diversity of corporate enterprise today makes it virtually impossible for any individual group to speak to the public or government with authority in behalf of the entire business community.

> *Organized labor speaks with one voice, while we speak with several.*

> *We do not have a unified voice for the free enterprise system itself, only for special interests.*

Business's Sense of Isolation

Businessmen see their inability to communicate with other social groups or the general public as a serious problem. Their sense of isolation seems to intensify their feeling of being misunderstood and unfairly abused. The chairman of one conference remarked,

> *We see ourselves as a persecuted few, while others see us as a privileged minority.*

Many executives commented on the insulation of chief executive officers: when they are not working with subordinates, they socialize with people of similarly high economic status who generally share their outlook and values.

> *When we visit a plant, we spend our time having drinks at the local country club, rather than mingling with workers.*

One executive suggested that, rather than complaining to the editor or publisher about an unfair article:

> *We should go out and have a beer with the reporters.*

There is awareness among some business leaders that they need to break out of their daily business and social routines and spend more personal time with other kinds of people—students, government officials, educators, who have a different conception of the business from their own. Yet they characteristically feel that they should *communicate to* these people, rather than listen to them. Most businessmen seem to think that their real problem is "getting through" to the public and that criticisms of business would evaporate once the business message reached the public's ears.

But there is a denser resistance that hampers business-public communications: business and the public inhabit different perceptual worlds. The executive's way of thinking about "his" institution is essentially economic and financial. For the businessman, the balance sheet and profit-and-loss statement connote restraint and discipline. Running a business is a risky venture, and the executive worries endlessly about anything that threatens his profits, and hence his survival. Even when the corporation itself is in danger, each quarter represents a challenge to the executive himself to produce profitable results—and, if possible, increasing profits.

For most critics of business, the span of concern goes far beyond the balance sheet or income statement. While the executive typically focuses on his company's profits and the market share of its products, the public perceives a business system or, at minimum, an industry—oil, autos, agriculture, grain dealerships, the banks, the railroads, chain stores, even "the media." Consumers tend to spread their dissatisfaction with one firm over many or all; business executives particularize and tend to isolate and minimize the poor performance or questionable behavior of individual firms.

Businessmen worry, first of all, about the level of their profits; consumers about the price and quality of the products they buy. Executives perceive themselves as relatively impotent, while consumers see themselves as impotent and large corporations as omnipotent.

For executives, profit is the prime source of efficiency; for much of the public, it is a tribute levied by the powerful on ordinary people. Executives see themselves as bravely performing in an extraordinarily harsh and dangerous environment; for most consumers and workers, it is the corporate executives who have it easy: they enjoy wealth and security, free from the constraints and job insecurity that affect ordinary citizens.

The business community's lack of touch with the perceptions and social attitudes of its critics is revealed by the concrete proposals for improving the public image of business suggested at the conferences, such as requiring courses in economics at the high-school level, using the corporation's contributions to higher education by rewarding those universities and colleges that offer a "balanced view of the free enterprise system" while withholding support from those "universities that graduate our foes," providing funds for a seminar to instruct college and university professors in the principles of a free enterprise system, and "getting together twenty of us to each contribute funds to buy a controlling interest in ABC so that at least one network will present a balanced viewpoint."

Such proposals, assuming that they could be implemented for the public-relations purpose their business proponents have in mind, seem more likely to reduce than to increase public support for the business system. What would be the impact on an academic faculty—the constituency whose goodwill is sought—of efforts by business to use its financial resources to influence the academic focus of universities? It would surely outrage the majority of professors who do not at all see the university as a bastion of anti-business sentiment, but rather of disinterested scholarship and learning; and it would confirm the fears of its most "paranoid" critics, already worried about protecting the university from being co-opted to serve corporate and government ends. Business would be charged with interfering with academic freedom and trying to impose its views on a free institution. An effort to take over a television network and run it on ideological right-wing principles would have a like effect—and would be of dubious legality under the FCC rules. There is, of course, no shortage of conservative newspapers; over 90 percent of the newspapers supported the Republican candidate in the 1972 election.

A similar communications gap is suggested by the call of

several executives at the conferences for increased political participation by citizens in order to insure that public officials are chosen by a more representative sample of the public. Particularly at those meetings immediately following the 1974 Congressional elections, many executives were upset by the low voter turnout in an election that produced the most liberal Congress in decades. "How many of you," asked one former executive currently serving in a high government position, "participated in last Tuesday's elections? That is the explanation for our defeat." Several executives urged their fellows to encourage their employees to participate more actively in politics and particularly to vote. Such statements reveal a lack of knowledge of American voting habits. The people who participate least in elections are those most likely to favor policies opposed by business. The lowest rate of voter turnout are among the poor, the blacks, and the young, and the highest are among the more affluent and highly educated, who tend to share a more conservative ideology.

The Legitimate Role of the State

The problem of executive insularity and insensitivity is very serious for an institution that correctly perceives that its autonomy and possibly even its survival rests on public approval and "consent." Just how real that danger is to corporations was revealed during the oil crisis of 1974, when much of the public—and Congress—became convinced that the great multinational oil companies had behaved irresponsibly, careless of public interests and preoccupied with their habitual profit-making goals. The oil industry is still feeling—

in very real terms, both legislative and pecuniary—the impact of that outburst of public distrust and anger.

However one judges the oil industry's policies, the oil crisis of 1974 demonstrates the necessity of a genuine effort by corporations to make their values and objectives congruent with those of society, and then of convincing the public that in fact they are. This is no easy task, especially for multinational corporations, which would like to be world citizens, but, since there is no world government and no "world community" to which they are responsible, they must plead loyalty to every country where they do business—even when those countries are in conflict with each other. In any case, as the late Hannah Arendt, the philosopher, wrote a generation ago:

> No matter what form a world government with centralized power over the whole globe might assume, the very notion of one sovereign force ruling the whole earth, holding the monopoly of all means of violence, unchecked and uncontrolled by other sovereign powers, is not only a forbidding nightmare of tyranny, it would be the end of all political life as we know it.[13]

The complexity of operating internationally obviously does not liberate corporate executives from the obligation of making social or moral choices. "There are few ways in which a man can be more innocently employed than making money," said Dr. Samuel Johnson; and this may hold for corporations as well as individuals most of the time. In their quest for profits, corporations doubtless increase economic efficiency—and the multinational corporations do this on a global scale.

Although some American corporations were once willing to do business with Hitler, or to subvert democratic government in Latin America and elsewhere—and there is nothing innocent about that—most are apolitical.

In any case, economics is not everything, and the nation-state, when it is healthy and principled, is the appropriate institution for setting and serving the broader social, political, and psychological goals of its citizens. To safeguard the freedom of its citizens, a nation cannot be the instrument of corporations that have no other purpose than profit maximization, however legitimate and useful that objective may be in a limited context.

The danger is not that corporations will pursue their pecuniary interests, especially if they do so within the constraints of competition, but that they may seek to corrupt and capture the powers of government and transfigure national values and institutions to serve corporate interests. Corporations that are insensitive to the needs and rights of any nation to determine its own social ends may be digging a grave for themselves. Any conflict between corporate autonomy and political freedom cannot be resolved by asserting the power of the corporation over that of the nation. Corporations that seek to do so are likely to produce a powerful social reaction against themselves.

What is needed, if both a free society and healthy economy are to be preserved, is a relationship between government and business that preserves the integrity of both institutions. If such a relationship between "power" and "property" is destroyed, "property will purchase power, or power will take over property. And either way, there must be an end to free government," as the prophetic Virginia statesman Benjamin Watkins Leigh warned, almost two centuries ago.

Or, as one conference participant put it in 1975,

> *Government without business is tyranny, and business without government is piracy.*

CHAPTER SEVEN

A Form of Elitism

MANY LEADING BUSINESS EXECUTIVES, feeling the intense political pressures upon them, have begun to wonder whether democracy and capitalism are compatible. Some are fearful of a shift in the power base to what some call "the masses":

A representative democracy has never worked in the history of the world and we are seeing that here. Autocracy has always followed democracy.

Maybe we should take the franchise away from government employees so the system can be restored.

One man, one vote will result in the eventual failure of democracy as we know it.

We are dinosaurs, at the end of an era. There is a shift of power base from industry and commerce to masses who cannot cope with the complexities of the modern world. Dolts have taken over the power structure and the capacity of the nation in the U.S. as well as in Western Europe.

Some businessmen are worried that democracy may be tenable only under conditions of abundance and growth, when there is little tension between corporate goals and public expectations. Under conditions of scarcity and stagnation, however, popular rule threatens to interfere with private capital accumulation and the effective functioning of the capitalist system. Many see a trend toward a more "authoritarian" or "controlled" system, inevitable if the corporation is to survive; some fear and oppose the trend; others are willing to accommodate themselves to it as a crisis-born necessity:

> To get through these hard times, government and business should assume a partnership of war-time proportions.

> We need hard war-time discipline. Unfortunately, we won't get it.

Most executives simply do not trust the public—and the politicians responsive to it—to control the economic decisions that affect their lives. They are afraid that the populace, suffering from "economic illiteracy," will squander resources on current public and private consumption and thus cripple capital formation and long-term economic growth. Businessmen perceive themselves as trustees for economic expansion and freedom; they, the affluent and productive, appreciate the meaning of scarcity and the importance of economic discipline.

In essence, business executives are modern Hamiltonians, heirs of Alexander Hamilton, the believer in government by an establishment of the informed, the propertied, and the responsible. A Hamilton champion, Herbert Croly, has said that "he [Hamilton] has been accused by his opponents of being the enemy of liberty; whereas in point of fact, he wished, like the Englishman he was, to protect and encourage liberty, just as far as such encouragement was compatible with good order, because he realized that genuine liberty would inevitably issue in fruitful social and economic inequalities." [1] However, where the Federalists justified their suspicion of democratic control in terms of an aristocratic faith in rule by the "wise, the rich, and the good," America's contemporary upper class puts greater emphasis on economic and managerial principles. Just as a firm cannot survive if all who work within it are rewarded equally and have equal authority, neither can a society.

Critics of the American system have long charged that "democracy stops at the factory gates"; what they may have failed to appreciate is how much the pattern of authority and reward within the firm becomes, for businessmen, the desirable model against which to compare political and economic relationships in the rest of the society. Within the firm, inequality is not only compatible with efficiency, it is critical for it, say American businessmen. Among American executives there has been relatively little interest in European experiments in and experience with "industrial democracy," or "co-determination." If democracy doesn't work for the firm, the most critical institution in all of society, American executives ask, how well can it be expected to work for the government of a nation—particularly when that government attempts to interfere with the achievements of the firm? The displeasure of businessmen increases as government becomes more responsive to nonbusiness pressures.

Authority relations within the firm, which the executive enjoys and seeks to safeguard, are a misleading guide to understanding the political process—and its frequent delays and frustrations. An executive is used to picking up the phone and getting things done. His subordinates may sometimes oppose and delay some of his plans, but he remains confident that ultimate formal authority remains vested in him. One cannot call up even a sympathetic Congressman, the head of an agency or a Presidential aide and tell him to "get things done." And often things don't get done at all. The decentralization of authority within the administration, as well as the separation of powers between the executive and legislative branches, assures that individual government officials or legislators are rarely in a position to "deliver." Most decisions must be approved by a wide number of individuals, contributing not only to delay, but assuring that the final outcome will reflect a process of bargaining rather than the consistency that results from command. But businessmen often underestimate the contribution of such political bargaining to the obtaining of "consent" and a workable (or at least enactable) program when power is widely dispersed among different constituencies.

The government's constituency is not only substantially wider than that of the corporation, but also the criteria of its performance are less clearly defined. Some businessmen are more understanding of the differences:

> *We are not a democracy in business. So we are on top, we are used to having our own way. We are, therefore, not used to dealing with the democratic process.*

> *You can't hope to dominate government completely. The best you can hope for are Congressmen who are open-minded.*

> *It didn't matter whether or not the public understood the tax laws as long as Wilbur Mills was around, but now public understanding has become more critical.*

And one executive wryly said that if he told a subordinate to jump out of a window, the only question he would get would be, "Which one?"

The Business Elite and the American Democracy

The persistent belief in a classless American society sometimes obscures the degree of suspicion and distaste with which the nation's financial "aristocracy" has long regarded democratic institutions and processes. The clear-eyed Tocqueville wrote in 1835:

> It is easy to perceive that the wealthy members of the community entertain a hearty distaste to the democratic institutions of their country. The populace is at once the object of their scorn and their fears.[2]

The business ideologies of the late nineteenth century, particularly Social Darwinism, were profoundly elitist and anti-democratic.[3]

According to historian Edward C. Kirkland, businessmen considered politicians "stupid, empty, noisy, demagogues," and the game of politics "managed by men who sought to devote themselves to it in order to gain a livelihood." Electoral majorities, in turn, were "brutal, selfish and ignorant." One businessman wrote in 1868,

In this good, democratic country where every man is allowed
to vote, the intelligence and the property of the country is
at the mercy of the ignorant, idle and vicious.

The viewpoint expressed by one business journal shortly before the opening of the Congressional session of 1880 sounds
remarkably current:

Activity is permeating every branch of business. In short,
the clouds have passed over, and the sun of prosperity is
once more shedding its benignant rays upon the United
States. Yet there is one little cloud still on the horizon—a
mere speck, it is true, but large enough to cause some
uneasiness. Congress is to assemble within a few weeks, and
the representatives of the people are busily engaged preparing their plans for the session. . . .[4]

Summarizing business thought in the 1920's, James
Prothro, professor of political science at the University of
North Carolina, concluded:

Properly wed to economic interests, vigorous and expanding
government may be praiseworthy. The conspicuous anti-
governmental orientation of business organizations is itself
an incident of the more basic fear that popular control will,
through the device of universal suffrage, come to dominate
the governmental process. Although economic success is
perfectly geared to the nature of man, political power is
dependent upon an artificial arrangement which runs directly
counter to the laws of nature and which gives full play to
the corruptibility of the masses. The unconscionable attempt
of the masses, misguided by parasitic politicians, to better

their lot through political processes constitutes the most unnerving of all the violations of fair play. Government is capable of meritorious service in the cause of "right," but politics as it is practiced in the twentieth century offers the constant threat of intruding the mass man's delusions into the social order.[5]

And as a conference participant said in 1975, expressing a widely held view among the corporate executives present at that meeting, although undoubtedly not the majority view of his peers nationwide:

> *Can we still afford one man, one vote? We are trembling on the brink.*

As executives are painfully aware, only a minority of the population considers itself members of the business community and identifies with its interests.

> *Since only a minority own the means of production, in a democracy, business will be a numerical minority.*

> *We don't have the votes. We have to achieve victories through organization and brains.*

> *We are seeing the lessening of power of wealth.*

However, despite the misgivings of business executives, long and particularly strong democratic traditions of the United States have probably worked to the advantage of business interests. Unlike Europe, where the struggle for the recognition of the rights of workers occurred simultaneously with demands for universal suffrage, America had universal suffrage (except for women and blacks) which was well-established before the industrial revolution created a working class. One result was that industrial conflict in America did not assume the political implications that it had in Europe; the legitimacy of the American political system was never seriously challenged by the "masses." American business has had less to fear from universal suffrage than any other business community in the world.

The American "working class," as represented by American unions, is, as businessmen recognize, more conservative than in any other modern capitalist nation. The United States is the only democratic nation without a significant socialist or workers' political party, and the socialist movement is far weaker in the United States than in Europe or Latin America among intellectuals, white-collar workers, young people, government employees, or small business people. Americans periodically become very critical of corporations, but their criticism has been within a populist, rather than socialist, framework.

The traditional role of the U.S. government in economic policy is that of umpire or helper rather than manager. Not only is the publicly managed sector relatively small in the United States, but many decisions that are made by government in all other countries are contracted out to business corporations.[6] Planning would go against a very deep American business tradition that assumes the incompetence of government responsibility for investment and production decisions. Apparently the only government activities that business feels comfortable with are contracting and subsidizing.

Americans tend to see their failures as personal rather than as the fault of the "system."[7] The enormous expansion of the consumer society since the 1920's has enabled the great majority of Americans to regard themselves as "middle class" and to substitute the ownership of homes, automobiles, and other durable consumer goods for productive property, and so to feel "propertied" rather than like a propertyless proletariat. The AFL-CIO president, George Meany, has himself said that the heavy assumption of mortgage and other debts and the need to pay college tuition bills for their children has had a very "conservative" impact on his union's membership.

Even with their elitist, anti-populist, and even anti-democratic bias, however, few American businessmen can fairly be regarded as "fascist," if by that term one means a believer in a political system in which there is a combination of private ownership and a powerful, dictatorial government that imposes major restrictions on economic, political, social, and religious freedoms. Basically, the anti-governmental mind set of the great majority of American businessmen has immunized them against the virus of fascism. The doctrine of "corporate social responsibility" emerged in the United States, precisely because it is seen by many businessmen as a way of *reducing* the role of the government in their affairs:

We have to think how we can meet new social demands without relying on government.

Social responsibility in the private sector is the alternative to regulation by the public sector.

We must assume responsibility for setting goals to preserve free enterprise. We don't want to trust the solution to government or unions.

Industrial States

John Kenneth Galbraith's concept of the "new industrial state," a term used to describe a joint corporate-government planning system, surely overstates the present structure and the identity of interest between business and government in the United States.[8] The "new industrial state" is less developed here than in any other major capitalist nation. Not only is corporate enterprise in the United States freer from state control and supervision, but American business and governmental elites share a degree of mutual mistrust equaled in few other nations. Compared to Japan or Germany, relatively few of the nation's major political leaders have business backgrounds.

Business and governmental elites in the United States are not united by the kind of "old boys' network" based on a common education, such as that provided by the Ecole Polytechnique in France, Oxbridge in England, or Todai in Japan. The United States lacks the easy and frequent interchange between middle- and upper-management positions that characterizes Japan and France. Even at Harvard, perhaps the closest American equivalent to the prestigious training grounds of the European business-governmental elite, prospective public and private officials are trained in separate facilities; the bridge over the Charles River connecting the Harvard Business School with the rest of the university is longer and narrower than it looks.

The populist charge about the domination of the United States government by business through bribes and illegal campaign contributions therefore misses the point. That corporations feel that they must give money to political officials to protect their interests is a sign of the distance of the ties between business and government, not their closeness; one does not have to bribe an "old boy" who naturally identifies with your interests. But to American businessmen, the federal government is remote from them:

> *Our problem is that Washington, D.C., is the only major capital that is not also a business center.*

Some years ago, Edward S. Mason, Professor of Economics at Harvard, observed:

> It is clear to the most obtuse observer that there is a much more distant relationship between business and government leadership in the United States, than, say, in Britain, France, or the Netherlands. . . . A British businessman can say, "Some of my best friends are civil servants," and really mean it. This would be rare in the United States.[9]

Andrew Hacker argues that business and legislative elites have different social outlooks based on distinctly different backgrounds and that these differences create a permanent tension between the legislators and the corporations in America:

> These tensions would not arise in such graphic form if the men who comprise the nation's political and economic elites were more similar in background and experience. While in no society can there be real homogeneity between these two groups, in a country like Great Britain political and eco-

nomic leaders are far more similar in character. For this reason, legislation affecting the British economy can secure political ends with a high degree of effectiveness and at the same time gain the approval of the corporate institutions which are directly affected. The American pattern, because it is more democratic, has been far less smooth in its operations.[10]

The anti-statist basis that has been so prominent in American business ideology for over a century contrasts vividly with the perspective of the European bourgeoisie. And on the American scene, the anti-government bias of business exceeds that of farmers, workers, educators, lawyers, and virtually every other group. Only doctors rival (or exceed) businessmen in their antipathy to the state.

In a sense, businessmen in the United States regard government in its present size and form as an upstart, an annoying and power-hungry Johnny-come-lately. The modern American "welfare state" can trace its development only from the 1940's; so the American bureaucratic state is less than half as old as the corporate bureaucracy. Again, the contrast with other capitalist nations is marked. In France and Japan, a strong state preceded the development of the modern corporation as well as the emergence of democratic forms and played a critical role in the creation of modern industry, while in Germany (Prussia) state and business corporation emerged simultaneously—and both before democratization. Compared to the French, German and Japanese states, the American government remains particularly open to citizen participation and peculiarly "inexperienced" in the management of a modern industrial society. In the United

States it was business, not government employment, that had all the best jobs, the money, and the prestige to offer.

The American businessman reached the zenith of his prestige in the 1920's. It is hard to imagine any American President today, even if he were a conservative and believed them, uttering Coolidge's celebrated 1925 remarks to a group of business executives for the record:

> You gentlemen come to speak for the interest that by far surpasses any other in the American community. This is a business country . . . and it wants a business government. I do not mean a government by business nor a government for business, but I do mean a government that will understand business.[11]

The Great Depression and the New Deal brought an end to that halcyon era for business. Virtually every force and tendency in American life that executives find disturbing is a product of the last four decades: a strong and interventionist state; big labor unions, virtually immune to corporate power; highly critical colleges and universities, and, most recently, strong civil rights, environmental, and consumer movements. American business still seems to be suffering from its precipitate fall from grace—and has not given up longing for the allegedly good old days.

Constrained Power

While the egalitarian ethic in American society—which contends that a business executive is no better than anyone else, just more successful and, hence, richer—helps to quell popular demands for radical changes in the business system, it also discourages the business community from assuming a position of moral and cultural leadership in the society. The pursuit of riches may or may not represent the least mischief that man is capable of, but it tends to require narrowly focused minds that are absorbed in the ten thousand and one details of day-to-day business affairs. The number of successful executives of impressive cultural accomplishments who have been unusually articulate in formulating a world outlook that transcends their daily preoccupations is very small.

The lack of a social ethic that accompanies "new money" has been dramatized by Mark Twain, William Dean Howells, Edith Wharton, Scott Fitzgerald, John O'Hara, and most recently, Joseph Heller. What we tend to forget is that in the United States "new money" is virtually all there is. And, lacking the authority that comes from widespread social approval, deference, and respect, corporate executives are driven to prove their right to high position and high income by their immediate economic performance. There seems little reason to quarrel with the judgment of Walter Lippmann:

> They give orders. They have to be consulted. They can more or less effectively speak for, and lead some part of, the population. But none of them is seated on a certain throne, and all of them are forever concerned as to how they may keep from being toppled off. They do not know how they happen to be where they are, although they often explain what are the secrets of success. They have been educated to achieve success; few of them have been educated to exercise power. Nor do they count with any confidence upon retaining their power, nor of handing it on to their sons. They live, there-

fore, from day to day, and they govern by ear. Their impromptu statements of policy may be obeyed, but nobody seriously regards them as having authority.[12]

But if individual corporate leaders are so lacking in real authority, how much power do their corporations really have?

The customary answer to that question by critics of the corporations usually begins with a statistical table showing what proportions of gross national product, or of manufacturing, or of selected industries are owned by the largest American corporations. Comparisons are made between the size of American Telephone & Telegraph or General Motors or Exxon and that of selected foreign countries or American states. Ten years ago Robert Heilbroner presented an awesome perspective by asking what would happen if the one hundred and fifty largest corporations disappeared overnight, by some selective catastrophe:

> To begin with, the nation would come to a standstill. Not only would the Union and the Southern Pacific, the Pennsylvania, the New York Central, and a half dozen of the other main railroads of the nation vanish, leaving the cities to starve, but the possibilities of supplying the urban population by truck would also disappear as the main gasoline companies and the tire companies—not to mention the makers of cars and trucks—would also cease to exist. Meanwhile, within the nine largest concentrations of urban population, all activity would have stopped with the termination of light and power, as the utilities in these areas vanished. In addition, communication in all these areas would break down with the disappearance of the telephone company.[13]

But that would be only the beginning. Virtually all steel production would stop, as would the production of the bulk of chemicals, electrical machinery, cars, trucks, tractors, and other farm implements. The food processors would be gone, together with the cans into which they put the food. Distribution patterns would collapse, and a national credit debacle would ensue. The insurance companies would vanish with $500 million in life insurance, effectively bankrupting a majority of American families.

To state the matter in that way, however, reveals the true limitations upon the power of these enormous enterprises. None of these corporations is seen to have the right to starve the cities, bankrupt the country, or prevent an individual from getting or using a telephone. Power in the United States is diffused among government agencies, labor unions, farm blocs, civil rights groups, individual citizens—all aware of their right to oppose and constrain the powers of great corporations. There is more than symbolic significance in the spectacle of a crusading Ralph Nader bringing to heel the General Motors Corporation, the Ford Motor Company, and the Chrysler Corporation, forcing them to recall hundreds of thousands of cars and spend millions of dollars. It should also be noted that Nader assailed the automotive giants with the help of a book-publishing corporation, the mass media supported by advertisers, the Congress, and the American legal system, which protected him from attempts of a few officials of the world's largest industrial corporation to harass him and invade his privacy in efforts to discredit him.

It is also worth noting that two of the corporate giants named by Professor Heilbroner—the Pennsylvania Railroad and the New York Central—after merging into the still gigantic Penn Central, collapsed into bankruptcy and have since been kept operating by the federal government. And it is further worth remarking that several of the great international oil companies on the list of one hundred and fifty largest corporations have since been bullied about and in some cases expropriated by relatively small nations in the Middle East, North Africa, and South America.

Nevertheless, it cannot be denied that large corporations do exercise considerable power over individual employees, suppliers, and customers, as well as through their influence on some elected legislators and public officials. Most clearly, they possess "market power" in the particular markets in which they operate, although this market power is moderated and countervailed by labor, farm groups, and other power blocs in the American system; by the Antitrust Division, the Federal Trade Commission, and other governmental regulatory agencies; and by the traditional pressures of competition, foreign as well as domestic, inter-industry as well as intra-industry. Those powerful corporations (such as the railroads, airlines, automobile manufacturers and big steel producers) that underrate inter-industry and foreign competitive pressures can still be badly hurt in the marketplace. American corporations do not like those hazards and pressures of competition today any better than they did in Adam Smith's day. One can safely expect that many American industries will continue to seek privileges, subsidies, tariffs, and other market protections from government; it will remain necessary for those concerned about the public interest to be on guard against unwarranted special favors to individual companies or industries by government.

Despite continuing pressures for monopoly, with or without

the help or collusion of government, the possibility for a basically liberal and competitive economic system to survive has been greatly enhanced since the 1930's by advances in economic theory and policy. The major weakness of the capitalist system has traditionally been its tendency to undergo wide swings from boom to bust, and this tendency has by no means disappeared, as recent events prove. But the progress in economics since the Depression makes one fairly confident that a similar national and international catastrophe can now be avoided by monetary and fiscal policies. A serious question remains, however, as to whether we will use intelligently what economic knowledge we have. Political opportunism and narrow, misguided self-interest may frustrate the sensible use of economic policy for preserving an environment of high employment and stable prices, so necessary to maintain an essentially free market economy.

The market economy, as it has evolved in the United States, evidently does not lend itself to the emergence of industrial dictators. Heilbroner, though worried about corporate power, says that, instead of corporate Caesars, "we are left with a largely faceless group known as 'management,' whose names the public neither knows or cares about." [14] In *The New Industrial State,* Galbraith agrees and suggests that corporate power has passed to a bureaucracy of technicians, "the technostructure." The prediction of a technocratic takeover was first made, of course, by Thorstein Veblen in 1919; he asserted that the "technologists" were discovering that together they constitute "the indispensable General Staff of the Industrial System" and could, "in a few weeks, incapacitate the country's productive industry." [15] Not any more in the United States than in the Soviet Union does that seem an actual possibility—because power lies elsewhere, and not only in government.

Many corporate board chairmen and presidents are far from powerless either outside or within their own organizations, and "the technostructure" does not make the most important business decisions nor provide its own leadership in corporations—nor wield much power in the broad society. American scientists and engineers are as far away today as they were half a century ago from taking control of the American economic system or the corporations in which they are employed. Technologists customarily strive to achieve power within the business world by making themselves into *businessmen,* rather than by remaining technicians. One route that leads in the direction of genuine corporate power is through graduate work in business or executive training programs paid for by their employers, and schools of business administration endow their graduates not with the values of a new technological superstructure but with the attitudes of the existing profit-oriented business management. Business management, on its side, does not fear the technologists; it needs all sorts of specialists to solve problems not only of production but of marketing, finance, and accounting and to cope with the corporation's labor, community, and government relations. Top management is pleased when a specialist shows that he is qualified for general managerial responsibility and has a highly developed sense of the importance of making money.

While American businessmen remain committed to profits and to economic growth, they are increasingly aware that economic growth and technological change can also produce social stresses and environmental threats that, if not wisely handled, could lead the broad public to conclude that these dangers outweigh the beneficial effects of industrial advance. Indeed, as a recent Harris poll discovered, by 61 percent to 23 percent, the public agreed with the statement that it was morally wrong for Americans to consume 40 percent of the world's energy and raw materials; by 81 percent to 10 percent, the public agreed that such consumption causes air and water pollution; and by 90 percent to 5 percent that we would have to cut back on "the amount of things we consume and waste." [16] In the face of such strongly held public attitudes—with majorities ranging up to 90 percent—American business is going to have to prove that it can be just as adaptable and imaginative socially and politically as it has been industrially if it is to avoid having far more serious curbs imposed upon its freedom of operation.

A failure of business to help solve the outstanding environmental and social issues of our time would indeed bring about the demise of business power. As the late A. A. Berle observed, "Power will invariably enter and organize any situation threatening chaos or disorder." [17] There have been moments in the recent past when the United States virtually ceased to be a workable society. The social breakdown expressed most tangibly in riots, crime, drug abuse, and urban decay has in fact caused the most serious anxiety among businessmen, whose deepest faith is that things must work, or, if they do not, that they must somehow be fixed.

To do the job that needs to be done, business must, however, achieve a new conception of its role in the society—and a new attitude toward what the society itself must do through government. In the past, the essence of American business power has been ideological—that is, it has provided the value conceptions and set the limits upon what the nation is doing or trying to do. Those conceptions must now be made more humane and sensitive to the needs and aspirations of all people. Ideological limits should not prevent us from using our matchless resources of energy and imagination for improving the conditions of life. If business plays its full role in this effort, it will help the society to avoid chaos and stagnation, on the one side, and an excessive concentration of power in the hands of government on the other.

But the insularity of business management and the intense but narrow focus of so many executives upon corporate objectives have hampered them from playing that role effectively. Perhaps inevitably, most businessmen project their own special perspective on the society at large; for them, the world is seen essentially as a marketplace, and the overriding objective of virtually everyone is considered to be personal gain. The corporate executive's understanding of the "hostility" toward business of the press, the academics, liberal politicians, and much of the public stems from the belief that these groups are merely pursuing their own self-interest, just as business executives do. Ironically, however, this appraisal does not cause businessmen to feel that they are just like every other group, or vice versa, but rather that businessmen are superior to the others. For, in the clash of interests between business and other groups, businessmen strongly believe that their own views should prevail, since they perform the crucial productive function for society, while all other interest groups are dependent on them, if not parasitic or predatory. As one business executive asserted:

> *Governments, unions, educational, religious and charitable organizations are consumers of capital, but have no independent resources to conduct economic activity and to participate in capital formation. We must use every resource at our command to make sure our citizens understand this. These institutions, and their employees, function on capital generated through taxes paid, and contributions made, either directly or indirectly with funds generated by business and its employees, both public and private.*

These other groups and institutions—which also want to see their views prevail—are seen as legitimate only to the extent that their goals complement, or at least do not interfere with, those of business.

In their conflicts with other groups, business executives do not simply want to prevail but to win the loyalty and allegiance of the others as well. Business, too, wants *converts* to its values and ideology. Executives plead for toleration and understanding, but what they really feel they merit is respect, admiration, and imitation. They often regard challenges to their interests and principles not as legitimate disputes and dissents in a pluralistic society, but rather as a threat to the system itself and to "freedom." To be an "economic illiterate" —in the eyes of many businessmen—is not simply to be ignorant but to be a heretic, an enemy of a healthily functioning economic and social order. (The "divine hand" cannot be relied upon to guide the economically illiterate, at least when politics enters the marketplace.)

Businessmen often feel that they are the elite who must

preserve the free enterprise system and the best interests of other groups in the society. No business executive today would say what the industrialist George Baer, president of the Reading Railroad, wrote in a famous letter at the beginning of the century:

> The rights and interests of the laboring man will be protected and cared for—not by the labor agitators, but by the Christian men to whom God in His infinite wisdom has given the control of the property interests of the country.[18]

—a statement that Baer himself lived to regret to the end of his days. Yet the instinctive (and quasi-religious) business elitism that underlies Baer's declaration persists. Executive opinion often appears on the verge of accepting government, labor, the universities, the press, and other groups as equal partners in the American polity and recognizing the importance of their contributions—as some businessmen actually do. But, for the most part, business executives never quite make their peace with these other institutions, so the "cold war" between business and society becomes a chronic condition. To be sure, there are phases of "detente," but when an economic crunch hits, executives are under attack—and they grow more defensive, and at the same time more aggressive against the politicians, the intellectuals, organized labor, or other perceived or imagined foes.

There is nothing new in all this. Business's tolerance of other groups does not progressively improve or worsen over the decades as much as it changes with the business cycle. Each new wave of prosperity promises to end the old animosities, but each wave of decline revives them.

To read through the hundreds of corporate statements on the social responsibilities of business during the earlier post-war prosperity is to be impressed with the sense of novelty and enthusiasm that pervades them. One would never suspect that most of these statements were identical in substance to statements issued by the business community fifty years earlier —or by intellectuals and publicists sympathetic to business and hopeful about the ability of corporations to assume broad social responsibilities. It was in January 1929—ten months before The Crash—that Walter Lippmann wrote:

> When the machine technology is really advanced, that is to say when it has drawn great masses of men within the orbit of its influence, when a corporation has become really great, the old distinction between public and private interests becomes very dim. I think it is destined largely to disappear. It is difficult even today to say whether the great railways, the General Electric Company, the United States Steel Corporation, the bigger insurance companies and banks are public or private institutions. When institutions reach a point where the direction is in the hands of salaried executives, technicians, and experts who hold themselves more or less accountable in standards of conduct to their fellow professionals, when the ultimate control is looked upon by the directors not as "business" but as a trust, it is not fanciful to say, as Mr. Keynes has said, that "the battle of socialism against unlimited private profit is being won in detail hour by hour." [19]

But it was fanciful to say so in 1929, just before a decade of turbulent labor relations and extreme business hostility toward government (and vice versa). Far-out and wishful statements about business's social role have periodically underrated the persistent tension between business and government in the United States. A decade ago Kenneth Boulding wrote:

> The most important current problem facing the United States economy is also a very old problem. This is the continued "cold war" between business and government, with organized labor and agriculture running interference for both, and increasing the noise level. This is something, of course, which has been going on since about 1880, but I think we have now got to the point where the failure to come to some kind of resolution of this ancient conflict is our most serious handicap, as it prevents the rational use of government power for the guidance of the economy and equally wastes the energy which business puts into it.[20]

Professor Boulding continued by putting the heaviest blame for this ancient conflict upon the business leadership of the country, which, he charges, has been "politically naive and obscurantist":

> It has failed to offer constructive criticism, which is desperately needed, of the impact of government on the economy. It has been almost as ideological in its own way as the Communists. It has failed to maintain adequate contacts with the intellectual community; and it has retreated into a closed subculture of its own. To some extent this can be explained by the trauma of the great depression, but it is surely time now to throw off the burden of this memory and to develop a business leadership which is capable of a realistic appraisal of its political and social environment.

But business does not yet seem ready to change its appraisal, as many comments at the 1974–75 conferences suggest:

> *The status and power of business has been preempted since World War II by unions, government, and academics.*
>
> *Why do we continue to contribute money to institutions that graduate our foes?*
>
> *Many liberal ideas come from the young. We contribute money to higher education, yet liberal professors produce liberal students. The free enterprise system is losing ground.*

An Estate—and The State

The concept of corporate social responsibility, curiously enough, may even impede understanding by businessmen of the role their organizations should play in a pluralist society, in which government plays the mediating and integrating role. In the famous *Federalist Paper No. 10,* James Madison explained that the coordinating legislative and administrative function of government was made necessary by "the various and unequal distribution of property":

> . . . Those who hold and those who are without property have ever formed distinct interests in society. Those who are creditors, and those who are debtors, fall under a like discrimination. A landed interest, a manufacturing interest, a mercantile interest, a moneyed interest, with many lesser interests, grow up of necessity in civilized nations, and divide them into different classes, actuated by different sentiments

and views. The regulation of these various and interfering interests forms the principal task of modern legislation, and involves the spirit of party and faction in the necessary and ordinary operations of the government.

The "advanced" business ideology which contends that corporate executives are responsible for "balancing" the competing interests of shareholders, workers, customers, and the general public bears a striking resemblance to Madison's description of the role to be played by the national government. But in point of fact, the corporation is structurally unsuited to this task: corporate officials do *not* represent the full diversity of interests that they affect in the broad society; only government can truly aspire to that role. The corporate "consent" creed notwithstanding, corporate executives are simply not accountable to the people in the same way politicians are—and businessmen do not want to be, if they can possibly avoid it. The interests of a business corporation do not necessarily represent the national interest, only a particular set of propertied interests, though these may have an important and widespread impact upon other interests—and upon the state.

The corporate executive's role is a combination of extraordinary impotence and potency. In some areas executives wield extraordinary powers, while in other areas they are the prisoners of economic and political forces beyond their individual control.

Even the market simultaneously encourages and frustrates the exercise of executive power: it gives wealth and control to those who master it, but it disciplines all who seek to gain from it, and can break those who blunder. Capitalism discovered a secret that had eluded all previous social systems—the secret of creating wealth. Yet the awesome potency of the system as a whole is commonly accompanied by a sense of impotence on the part of the capitalists themselves, especially in hard times.

Politics, which businessmen understand less than they do the market—and for which they have less talent—intensifies their anxieties. The outstanding philosopher—and admirer—of capitalism in the twentieth century, Joseph Schumpeter, has devastatingly described the curious mixture of strength, weakness, and narrowness of economic focus that hurts the businessman as social and political leader:

> . . . There is surely no trace of any mystic glamour about him which is what counts in the ruling of men. The stock exchange is a poor substitute for the Holy Grail. We have seen that the industrialist and merchant, as far as they are entrepreneurs, also fill a function of leadership. But economic leadership of this type does not readily expand, like the medieval lord's military leadership, into the leadership of nations. On the contrary, the ledger and the cost calculation absorb and confine.
>
> I have called the bourgeois rationalist and unheroic. He can only use rationalist and unheroic means to defend his position or to bend a nation to his will. He can impress by what people may expect from his economic performance, he can argue his case, he can promise to pay out money or threaten to withhold it, he can hire the treacherous services of a *condottiere* or politician or journalist. But that is all and all of it is greatly overrated as to its political value. Nor

are his experiences and habits of life of the kind that develop personal fascination. A genius in the business office may be, and often is, utterly unable outside of it to say boo to a goose—both in the drawing room and on the platform. Knowing this, he wants to be left alone and to leave politics alone.[21]

The corporation alone is incapable of looking out for the corporate system or the political system. That requires, as James Madison suggested, a combination of several "factions" —including a relatively small number of unusually able, thoughtful, and articulate businessmen through whom the interests and contribution of business as a whole can become better understood, appreciated and employed for the welfare of the society as a whole.

CHAPTER EIGHT

The Need for a Transcendent Ideology—and a Personal Ethic

AMERICAN BUSINESS EXECUTIVES today are deeply concerned over the loss of public respect for business and the loss of their ability to provide leadership in the American society.

How can these be regained? Some executives feel that the first step is for businessmen honestly to reexamine what has gone wrong, and why—and to what extent business itself has caused public hostility by its negligence, improper behavior, and failure to address itself seriously and disinterestedly to the crucial problems facing the broad society. One leading executive, Stanley Marcus, chairman of Neiman-Marcus of Dallas, contends that business is very much to blame for its own troubles:

> There is a massive loss of faith in the business community by the American people—and perhaps a loss of faith on the part of businessmen as well.
> Let's not kid ourselves into believing that the negative attitude toward business is merely part of an "anti-Establish-

ment" mood throughout the nation. It is a lot more justified than that.

Americans still believe in the free-enterprise system. They have no quarrel with profit-making. But they do have a quarrel with unethical and questionable business practices conducted at the public expense.

They do have a quarrel with companies which pollute our water and air and are apparently indifferent to the hazards of pollution until the Government intervenes.

They do have a quarrel with that majority of businessmen who have fought and obstructed and delayed every piece of progressive legislation enacted during this century.

Who among the business community today would seriously propose that Congress repeal our child-labor laws— or the Sherman Antitrust Act? The Federal Reserve Act, the Securities Exchange Act? Or workman's compensation? Or Social Security? Or minimum wage? Or Medicare? Or civil rights legislation?

All of us today recognize that such legislation is an integral part of our system; that it has made us a stronger, more prosperous nation—and, in the long run, has been good for business. But we can take precious little credit for any of the social legislation now on the books, for business vigorously opposed most of this legislation.

I wonder sometimes if we really believe in the free-enterprise system. When those who have the greatest stake in it often turn out to be its greatest enemies, I wonder if free enterprise can survive.

Can it survive when some of its greatest proponents seem determined to strangle the life force of the system—competition—with such practices as collusive bid-rigging and price-fixing?

Can free enterprise survive inaccurate, misleading, or "unexplained" financial reporting? Or auditors who violate their code of ethics to help companies falsify financial statements and perpetrate massive swindles, running into the hundreds of millions of dollars, that involve inflated assets, sales and earnings, fraudulent insurance policies, nonexistent securities, and the collection of death benefits on coverage that never existed?

What are we to think—not just of the executives behind the fraud and the auditors who helped them—but of the dozens of employees who knew about the fraud but did nothing, and the powerful investors who benefited from the inside information?

Can free enterprise survive companies which flout the law by making illegal political contributions with corporate funds? Is it any wonder that 53 percent of our population believes that the large corporations should be broken up when they read that in 1972 seven companies alone contributed nearly a half-million dollars to the Committee to Reelect the President?

It does no good to try to justify these contributions—as some have done—as the cost of doing business with the Government. Other companies *refused* to give—and they're still in business.[1]

But many other businessmen would find this too harsh an indictment.

Corruption and Confusion

Within that amorphous group, the American business community, there is a wide spectrum of social and moral attitudes, which the following quotations from the conferences suggest:

> *Half your wives are involved in activities you wouldn't support.*

> *Formerly we had power—our goals and values were in the mainstream.*

> *There is reason for us to be criticized. We have been too preoccupied with profit and have not adequately anticipated public expectations.*

> *The heads of the institutions set the tone for their organizations. We are not adequately insisting on morality from the top.*

> *How can you control some twelve to twenty levels below you if you can't control your own children?*

> *We shouldn't take advantage of people who cannot take care of themselves.*

> *Perhaps we should adopt Blumenthal's [W. Michael Blumenthal, chairman of Bendix] suggestion and establish a code of ethics for businessmen, like the ones for lawyers and doctors.* (Voice from across the room: *You mean one that would work as well as the Bar Association's?*)

Many executives held that business was no worse than any other element in the society in its moral standards, and that the problem was just a familiar condition of life.

> *The immorality of business and government are not worse than in the past, just more visible.*

Immorality in business is just like crime in the streets. It will never be eliminated.

Every time I have a pure competitive instinct, my lawyer tells me, "Try it and they will put you away."

The fact that Lockheed has bribed some sheik to buy airplanes doesn't bother me a bit.

But not all agreed. Some thought the situation had worsened:

There is a general deterioration of moral standards. Business reflects this deterioration and contributes to it.

We all use the jackal technique of management selection— hold the red meat over the pack and see who can jump the highest.

Business [obscenity deleted] all the time in TV ads. Most business communication takes place via silly advertising. This weakens our credibility.

Most businessmen think their competitors are as immoral as the critics of business think they are.

Some businessmen blamed the moral decline they perceived on institutions other than business:

Government—what can I say about the moral tone of government, ranging from the knowingly inflated campaign promises through the smothering blanket of mindless bureaucracy to out-and-out corruption, that you have not already heard or experienced ad nauseam? I shall only add that the confusion between legality and morality, between pragmatism and principle, already nurtured by the churches

> *and the university, reaches new levels in the day-to-day*
> *workings of all levels and nationalities of government.*

Some emphasized the decline of organized religion—and the "politicization" of the churches:

> *I believe that a major contribution to the decline in business*
> *morality and ethics is the decline in the influence of the*
> *major religions, and the concurrent switch to "situational*
> *ethics." For centuries, it seems to me, the churches served*
> *as impregnable standard-bearers—as delineators of generally*
> *accepted boundaries that could not be crossed without*
> *recognition of wrong-doing. Today the churches no longer*
> *serve the function—they are of the battle and not above it*
> *—politicized, strident, and internally divided. . . .*

Others felt that moral leadership was lacking not only in the churches, but also in the family, government, the schools:

> *In our society the moral and value-judgment leadership*
> *which fifty years ago was substantially provided by the*
> *churches has been substantially eroded. It has not been*
> *replaced by stronger families, by our system of government,*
> *or by our educational institutions. There is a great moral-*
> *leadership vacuum today.*

One executive suggested that, especially among the young, traditional morality had given way to vague concepts of social justice—which rationalized *immorality:*

> *History becomes what has happened in the past six months,*
> *selectively extracted. Morality becomes rationalization of*

criminal behavior in the diffused illumination of social injustice. And the logical process begins with the conclusion firmly in place and the premises still to be found or fabricated.

But many businessmen are far from feeling self-righteous or secure in their own moral beliefs. Some consider that young people today are searching for better answers in an age when the traditional values have eroded or collapsed:

My children's generation is educated to ask questions whereas I learned to memorize answers. They question deeply and sincerely the basic fairness of our socio-economic system and yearn for changes to improve it. They have been cast adrift from the relatively simple values of patriotism, the Ten Commandments, the sanctity of marriage, and so on, without substitute values. They subscribe to situation ethics but decry the morality of government and business leaders. They reject materialism but demand more material for all. I could go on endlessly to describe a generation moving into their productive lives long on information, speculation, desire for change—confused about their personal goals—and short on certitude about basic values and moral principles.

Some argued that whatever the stresses and strains, the business community as a whole still held to traditional moral principles, although there have been flagrant exceptions. Most would reject the kind of overall indictment made by the novelist Saul Bellow: "Under Nixon the great corporations became drunk with immunity. The good old bourgeois virtues, even as window dressing, are gone forever." One executive said:

*It is unfair to blame twelve million businesses in the United
States for the unethical behavior of a few score.*

Another insisted that politics—and political fund-raising—
were inherently crooked and always had been.

Several executives frankly acknowledged that business had
a heavy economic stake in influencing the political process
and that this was the root cause of illegal political contributions:

*There is a problem of moral stamina. When it came down to
Nixon or McGovern, the outcome really meant a lot. This
was the fundamental reason for illegal political actions.*

Many business executives felt that the only way to deal
with the problem of stopping dishonest or illegal corporate
behavior was for top management itself to adopt high standards, make these crystal clear to everyone below them, and
then lay down the line in unmistakable terms.

Said one businessman:

*The highest code is something like that expressed by Irwin
Miller of Cummins Engine who called his top management
together, after the American Airlines' illegal political
contribution was disclosed, to reiterate his policy of "100
percent adherence to 100 percent honesty, even if we lose
by it." ...*

*Miller's way may not only be shorter but better. When it
comes to immoral behavior that may benefit the corporation,
such as payoffs, the record of opposition is considerably
less than 100 percent, although, moral standards aside, there
is a lot of truth in the street wisdom that once you start to
pay all you can do is pay more. Gulf made payoffs of close to*

*$500,000 to the President of Bolivia to prevent expropria-
tion by a successful regime. Now that the bribe has been
disclosed, the new regime has said it will withhold over $50
million still due Gulf in indemnity.*

This man said he knew top-management support was crucial to honest behavior within the firm—and cited his own
experience:

*With top management support, almost all pressures,
including societal, can be resisted, but without it you are in
need of deliverance. I once had to obtain a building permit
to build a cement silo in greater Chicago. In three communities—one after another—I was asked for a $5,000
payoff by either the mayor or the building inspector. A
major Chicago law firm to which I turned for legal help said
there was no recourse except the payoff, which they of
course would not handle, but they would give me the name
of a lawyer who would, billing it as a service. Our sales
department gave me to understand they wanted the silo now,
not tomorrow, and whatever had to be done to get the
permit should be done. I was fortunate on two counts. The
president was an Irwin Miller type, and before too long I
obtained the permit legally in a community where a citizen-
reform ticket had just thrown the syndicate out of power.
Business morality, as so many of you have pointed out, is
rarely higher than that made visible by top management.*

But top management needs to do more than make high
moral standards visible; it must "inspect for compliance":

*Since the inspection process must be limited, it should occur
at the pressure points in the organization. Are the weaknesses*

of your organization at the top management level, middle, or lower? Is the weakness likely to be from the outside—suppliers bribing your purchasing agents? Or from the inside—your salesmen bribing customers, your inspectors falsifying records? Is the weakness societal or is society supportive of business morality?

Some business executives believe that public standards of business morality are rising, at least in the United States, and expect this process to continue.

One executive saw no need for businessmen to obscure the real issue by acting as though they were discussing some profound philosophical issue:

What we are talking about is inhibiting lawbreaking—certainly the minimum standard that is going to be imposed on publicly held corporations—or inhibiting the breaking of codes of conduct more strict than law.

There is great reluctance among business executives to "name names" or publicly criticize other businesses for illegal actions—whether because of fear of a loss of business, concern about "washing our dirty linen in public," anxiety about being "kicked out of the club," or loathness to claim moral superiority and the right to censure others. Yet there is recognition that businessmen's silence on the transgressions of other businesses have contributed to a general public belief that "they're all alike" or "they're all in this together." However, at one of the conferences in the fall of 1975, a business executive forthrightly began his statement on "business morality" by saying:

Exxon yesterday disclosed some $50 million of foreign bribes in its registration statement and has promised to stop the practice. The SEC is suing Westinghouse for having lied to its employees and the public by saying that its Appliance Division was not for sale when in fact they were in the last stage of negotiation with White Consolidated. My gut feeling is that American business is divided about evenly between businesses that will be forced to raise standards and those that already attempt to operate to standards that are higher than anything the public can impose.

There was little cant on the subject of business morality during the conferences. Some executives said that business results—and survival—inevitably came first:

It is as true of companies as it is of man that it is easier to be moral when you are successful than when your back is to the wall.

If we wait until all businessmen are ethical before we start our sales job, we will never get started.

A few argued that executives' responsibility to the economic survival of institutions sometimes dictated that they violate the law; if they did not, their stockholders would suffer, and other firms "with less scrupulous management" would win out (a rationalization common among politicians and national leaders charged with illegal or immoral behavior).

Many business executives assert that, whatever their personal views or preferences, their primary responsibility must be to their firm and its financial interests. Thus, while insisting that they believe in free enterprise or democratic principles, executives often insist that they have no right to refuse to trade with the Soviet Union or other communist countries, or to refuse to invest in South Africa, Peru, Chile, or other countries that violate human rights, or to refuse to cooperate with Arab countries that insist on religious discrimination—provided that their actions are held to be legal by the United States Government and that they are perceived by business executives as furthering their own companies' interests. Trade and investment with countries whose policies we disapprove of, the executives often say, may yet do some good by improving friendship with our country, breaking down prejudice, promoting development of the world economy; in any case, our job is not to make moral decisions, which are highly subjective, but to make money for our companies. The nation makes the laws and determines the national policies—we should respect those laws, but we are not required to go beyond them, any more than in paying our income taxes. Further, say many executives, if we give up the business in a country we don't like, another company will simply take it over, and what good will it do?

Business executives, according to such arguments, have no right to wrap themselves in the mantle of moral philosophers and judges—especially to the detriment of the interests of their shareholders whose money they are using; and this, many say, is as true on domestic as on foreign issues.

One executive who had been reading *The Morality of Consent* by the late Alexander Bickel, professor of law at Yale, was impressed with his contention that "morality threatens to engulf us." Professor Bickel wrote, with particular reference to the law:

The legal order has heaved and groaned for years under a prodigality of moral causes and, if not broken, it is no wonder that it is badly bent. Vietnam, let us not forget, was not only a moral error but, for its authors, a moral urgency. The urgencies of "peace with honor," of the clean life, of patriotism—in a word, Watergate—were merely the last straws. It is ironic, but entirely natural, that "law-and-order" as a moral imperative should have clashed with the legal order. For the legal order, after all, is an accommodation. It cannot sustain the continuous assault of moral imperatives, not even the moral imperative of "law-and-order," which as a moral imperative has only a verbal resemblance to the ends of the legal order.

No legal order can sustain such a bombardment, and the less so a federal constitutional order of separated and diffused powers. It is the premise of our legal order that its own complicated arrangements, although subject to revolutionary change, are more important than any momentary objective. This premise must give way at times to accommodate inevitable change. Change which is significant, as Justice Brandeis once wrote, manifests itself more "in intellectual and more conceptions than in material things." But our legal order cannot endure too rapid a pace of change in moral conceptions, and its fundamental premise is that its own stability is itself a high moral value, in most circumstances the highest. The legal order must be given time to absorb change, to accommodate it to itself as well as itself to it. If the pace is forced, there can be no law.[2]

Some businessmen feel this reasoning applies, *a fortiori,* to business institutions; as one executive put it, public demands for "moral" behavior "may be another rack on which business is stretched."

> *And like Salem's witches, we concede our guilt, first because moralists are so imperative, and it's easy and appealing short term to plead guilty or at least* nolo contendere, *but most fundamentally because we have no moral code to repair to and because, in the sunshine, many of our actions do seem immoral by ancient standards.*

Yet businessmen recognize, as Professor Bickel also did, that the existing order of laws or business practices "must give way at times to accommodate inevitable change," and that this is probably one of those times. A business executive concluded:

> *What to do? Well, as they say, the pendulum swings, water seeks its own level, and plastic substances deform under pressure. Likewise, business morality will, even without an act of conscience, move to conform to its changing environment. But I believe we desperately need a massive, positive act of conscience and will—to search out, define, disseminate and* practice *a renewed set of moral principles.*

The issue of business morality is, and cannot avoid being, both a personal and an institutional matter for every corporate executive and for every employee who does not mean to surrender his individual integrity, his honor, his very soul, to an organization. The twentieth century has witnessed far too many horrible examples, not just in business, but in politics and within military organizations, of individuals who surrendered their moral judgments to the control and value systems of their organizations, the archetypical case being that of Adolf Eichmann, the bureaucratic functionary par excellence.

The issue of how to achieve responsible and decent moral judgment and moral behavior from those who serve large organizations cannot be solved, however, just at the personal level. It necessarily involves organizational values and their implementation. Relatively few men or women are heroes; the everyday behavior of most people reflects the values of their organizations, especially as defined at the top. This is why it is so crucial to a decent society that those who head large corporations—and influence the laws and practices of the society as well—be persons of firm and deep moral principle. Business executives cannot divorce themselves from their moral obligations by saying that they have an obligation only to live within the laws of the land; they themselves are important factors in determining what those laws will be. The problems at the state level are as critical as those in Congress. And these executives certainly have heavy responsibilities that they cannot avoid for shaping the moral principles that affect their own business organizations. They frequently have more leeway than some businessmen are willing to admit in shaping their companies' external actions, both domestically and internationally, and they could find considerable support among their various constituencies, if they sought it, for intelligent and at the same time morally responsible and sensitive corporate policies.

Beyond Self-interest

A business community, if it is to assume a position of leadership in society, must somehow generate a vision of purpose that transcends its own role and its own direct and immediate benefits. But such a transcendent vision is extremely difficult for American businessmen to attain, since it appears to conflict with the traditional and deepest American ideology, to which Alexis de Tocqueville, a century and a half ago, gave the name "the philosophy of self-interest." Today, as when the Republic was still young, Americans generally deny that they ever behave altruistically. In this respect, Tocqueville said that Americans often failed to do justice to themselves; although he found that the Americans, like people everywhere, sometimes give way to "those disinterested and spontaneous impulses that are natural to man," he said that Americans seldom would "admit that they yield to emotions of this kind; they are more anxious to do honor to their philosophy than to themselves." [3]

One of the reasons that the traditional American ideology, of which American businessmen are the principal conservators, is so inhibiting is that it is too narrowly *economic*. The philosopher Alfred North Whitehead clearly perceived the dangers—to society and to business itself—of focusing on abstract economic principles rather than on social, political, and moral principles as well. He linked the constricting nature of the traditional business ideology to the faults of an archaic economic doctrine, and even of modern science itself, with its useful but distorting abstractions. And Whitehead argued for a more holistic and organic conception of social institutions, whether at the factory level or for the society as a whole:

A factory, with its machinery, its community of operatives, its social service to the general population, its dependence upon organizing and designing genius, its potentialities as a source of wealth to the holders of its stock is an organism exhibiting a variety of vivid values. What we want to train is the habit of apprehending such an organism in its completeness. It is very arguable that the science of political economy, as studied in its first period after the death of Adam Smith (1790), did more harm than good. It destroyed many economic fallacies, and taught how to think about the economic revolution then in progress. But it riveted on men a certain set of abstractions which were disastrous in their influence on modern mentality. It de-humanized industry. This in only one example of a general danger inherent in modern science.

This is also the case with business. American businessmen today are facing the necessity of transcending a particular form of rationalism which has gone stale and become limiting, dangerous, and anti-rational, as Whitehead described science. He saw a need for change, but change melded with conservation:

> There are two principles inherent in the very nature of things, recurring in some particular embodiments whatever field we explore—the spirit of change, and the spirit of conservation. There can be nothing real without both. Mere change without conservation is a passage from nothing to nothing. . . . Mere conservation without change cannot conserve.[4]

By clinging to an outmoded ideology, American businessmen and their political representatives are trying to impose solutions that not only fail, but also impede more effective means of dealing with national and international problems, such as inflation and unemployment, poverty and the mal-distribution of income, the decay of cities, environmental deterioration, the shortage of food and other vital resources, and the energy crisis. It is this failure to solve crucial prob-lems which, as Professor George Cabot Lodge has ably argued, is really undermining the legitimacy of corporations and threatening their autonomy. Professor Lodge defines the traditional American ideology as consisting of five great ideas: individualism, property rights, competition, the limited state, and scientific specialization and fragmentation. He sees this doctrine giving way to a new American ideology, with five quite different elements: "Communitarianism," the idea that if the community is well designed, its members will have a sense of identity with it; rights of membership in the community to survival, income, health, and other basic needs; community needs and purposes as the means of justifying or controlling the use of property; the state as a planning agency for the society, setting goals and arbitrating conflicting needs; holism, the theory of the interdependence of elements, replac-ing scientific specialization and fragmentation.[5] Surveys by Professor Lodge and William F. Martin find that more than two-thirds of businessmen prefer the traditional American ideology although many "sense its replacement by a new set of value definitions based on communitarian principles." Some 62 percent of the respondents regarded the traditional ideology as the more dominant in the United States today, but 72 percent thought new values would dominate in 1985.[6]

Many American businessmen, while still wedded by habit, emotion, and their immediate economic interest to the old-time religion of free enterprise, are coming to recognize that it is becoming increasingly difficult to practice that religion in the present stage of economic, social, and political development. Much of this nation and much of the world refuse to accept profit-seeking as the sole arbiter of business conduct or resource use. Therefore, more and more thoughtful business executives, whether because they think it is prudent and necessary or because they think it is right, are trying to form a new philosophy or ideology; or, to put it more plainly, to find a new way of conceiving of their job, of their role, of their mission, of their values, that might lead to a better reconciliation of private objectives and public goals. Their hope is to find a means of safeguarding the relative autonomy of private business while helping to solve urgent public problems which large corporations cannot help but affect one way or the other—for good or evil.

While the overriding issue is to redefine the relationship of the corporation to the commonweal, the real difficulty is to work out the specific issues that need to be solved and to find the specific institutions, private or public, or private *and* public together, that can do the job of coping with the most critical issues. Those issues will change from time to time; and the political-economic system must be made more responsive to changing problems, and quicker in its responses. The energy problem is just one example of how slow the American system has been in responding to a clear economic and political danger; the energy problem was perceived years before the political system could make an adequate response —and indeed it has still not done so. The problem of decaying central cities is a second case in point. And virtually every problem on the national agenda falls into that category. Not only must we have better answers to the problems themselves, which means making the fullest and best use of our intellectual resources, but we must improve our political-economic system in such a way as to cut down the time lag between when a major problem is perceived and when an effective solution is developed and launched.

If there are to be timely solutions to the sorts of problems facing the United States and the entire world, solutions on which the future of civilization and human existence itself depends, there will have to be contributions from many sectors—from the sciences, from the social sciences, from the humanities, from labor, from agriculture, from political institutions, and from business as well.

But something more will be required if the critical problems are to be solved. Most of all, we must have respect and concern for other people—in our own country and in other countries—a genuine and deep morality, which is the attribute of the human race that substitutes for the survival instinct of other animals. If that morality, personal and social, within political as well as business institutions, should atrophy or be seriously attenuated, our problems may become insoluble. Walter Lippmann said it very well a generation ago:

> The wisdom deposited in our moral ideals is heavily obscured at the present time. We continue to use the language of morality, having no other which we can use. But the words are so hackneyed that their meanings are concealed, and it is very hard . . . to realize that virtue is really good and really relevant. Morality has become so stereotyped, so thin and verbal, so encrusted with pious fraud, it has been so much monopolized by the tender-minded and the senti-

mental, and made so odious by the outcries of foolish men and sour old women, that our generation has almost forgotten that virtue was not invented in Sunday schools but derives originally from a profound realization of the character of human life.

This sense of unreality is, I believe, due directly to the widespread loss of genuine belief in the premises of popular religion. Virtue is a product of human experience: men acquired their knowledge of the value of courage, honor, temperance, veracity, faithfulness, and love, because these qualities were necessary to their survival and to the attainment of happiness.[7]

As for the survival of business institutions and the values of independence and liberty that businessmen cherish, these depend not just on profits but on a broader and deeper conception of the public good.

Conservation and Change

Thus the issue of personal morality overlaps that of the social and political policies of corporate executives. The least well-kept secret about business is that the overwhelming majority of corporate executives are conservative, well to the right of the majority of Americans. It would be astonishing if this were not so, since corporate executives, with their high incomes, considerable wealth, and responsibility for protecting and increasing the size and profits of the organizations they manage, have a powerful vested interest in "conserving" the capitalist system.

Yet the most politically and socially astute business leaders do recognize that, to preserve the system, they must change, their institutions must change, and capitalism itself must change in response to new objective conditions and to new social demands. Such conservatives recognize that they will lose all if the system fails—and that excessive rigidity or negativism on the part of business can result in systemic failure.

This recognition does not require the abandonment of an essentially conservative ideology. Indeed, a free society needs the support of a truly conservative ideology—one that demonstrates particularly the dangers of too powerful, too pervasive, and too costly a state apparatus and bureaucracy, which are themselves very likely to become the foes of moral principle.

To command significant public support, however, a conservative ideology must provide a better defense of limited government than that of preserving the economic freedom, privileges, prerogatives, wealth and power of corporations and their managers or owners.

Notes

CHAPTER ONE

1. *The Wall Street Journal,* on Feb. 2, 1976, reported that much polling evidence indicated that "alienation and cynicism toward politics and government have become pervasive after a confidence-shattering decade stretching from Vietnam through Watergate and a deep recession." Items:
   - By a margin of almost two to one, a Caddell poll finds that people believe "most politicians don't really care about me."
   - 58 percent believe that "people with power are out to take advantage of me," according to the Louis Harris Survey.
   - 49 percent believe that "quite a few of the people running the government are a little crooked," according to Market Opinion Research Inc., used by President Ford's campaign.
   - 68 percent feel that "over the last ten years, this country's leaders have consistently lied to the American people," according to a Caddell poll.
   - 57 percent believe that "both the Democratic and Republican parties are in favor of big business rather than the average worker," according to a survey by Peter Hart, a pollster for many Democrats.
2. Clifford Geertz, "Ideology as a Cultural System," in David E. Apter, *Ideology and Discontent* (New York: Free Press, 1964), p. 53.

CHAPTER THREE

1. Fletcher L. Byrom, "Public Affairs, Private Business and People," *Conference Board Record,* May 1975, p. 52. Mr. Byrom quotes

Marshall Wright, an executive of Eaton Corporation and former Under Secretary of State:

> There is good reason to suspect that the American political system is proving itself increasingly incapable of responding to its challenges, that there are serious institutional distortions in the way in which our system is supposed to work.

2. Robert Lindsey, "Henry Ford Asks U. S. Plan to Avert Economic Crisis," *New York Times,* Dec. 10, 1974, p. 77.

3. "The Case for Government Planning," *New York Times,* Sect. 3, p. 14, March 15, 1975.

4. Arjay Miller, "The Social Responsibility of Business," address delivered at White House Conference on the Industrial World Ahead, Washington, D. C., Feb. 7–9, 1972.

5. Robert V. Roosa, "National Economic Planning," statement to the Joint Economic Committee of Congress, Nov. 13, 1975.

6. Byrom, "Public Affairs," *op. cit.,* p. 54.

7. This is the major theme of Theodore Lowi's book, *The End of Liberalism* (N.Y.: W. W. Norton, 1969), as well as Grant McConnell's *Private Power and American Democracy* (N.Y.: Alfred A. Knopf, 1966).

8. R. G. Tugwell and E. C. Banfield, "Governmental Planning at Mid-Century," *Journal of Politics,* May 1951, pp. 133–63. Robert Engler, *The Politics of Oil* (Chicago: Univ. of Chicago Press, 1961). Michael Reagan, *The Managed Economy* (N.Y.: Oxford University Press, 1963), Bertram Gross, "National Planning: Findings and Fallacies," *Public Administration Review,* Dec. 1965, pp. 263–73.

9. Andrew Hacker, "Citizen Counteraction," in *Corporate Power in America,* ed. Ralph Nader and Mark J. Green (N.Y.: Grossman Publishers, 1973), p. 176.

10. "Linking Up," in *IPS Transactional Link,* August 1975, a publication of the Institute for Policy Studies, a radical think tank in Washington, D.C.

11. Publication No. 6, October, 1975, Proceedings of a Seminar at Washington University, Center for the Study of American Business, September 11, 1975.

12. Quoted in John Minahan, "Is 'Free Market' A Dirty Word?" *Saturday Review,* July 12, 1975, pp. 18, 19.

13. Leonard Silk, *Nixonomics,* (N.Y.: Praeger, 1972 and 1973).

CHAPTER FOUR

1. Max Ways, "A Hall of Fame for Business Leadership," *Fortune,* Jan. 1975, pp. 64–73, 168.
2. "The Top Man Becomes Mr. Outside," *Business Week,* May 4, 1974, p. 39.
3. Rawleigh Warner, Jr., "On Becoming 'A Controversial Issue of Public Importance,' " *Conference Board Record,* August 1974, p. 3.
4. This is the credo of *The New York Times,* published on the editorial page on August 19, 1896, when Adolph Ochs took over the paper; oddly enough, it ran under the heading "Business Announcement."
5. From Field Research Corporation, 1975.
6. "The Public Mandate for Business," presented at Public Affairs Conference of the NICB, April 21, 1966.
7. Thomas C. Cochran, "Business and the Democratic Tradition," *Harvard Business Review,* March–April 1956, p. 41.
8. S. M. Lipset, *Commentary,* July 1975, p. 59.
9. Katherine Graham, "On the Quality of the Press," *Conference Board Record,* April, 1975, p. 42.
10. William H. Whyte, Jr., *Is Anybody Listening?* (N.Y.: H. Wolff Book Co., 1950), pp. 3–4.

CHAPTER FIVE

1. D. W. Brogan, *The American Character* (N.Y.: Alfred A. Knopf, 1944), pp. 25, 29.
2. Louis Harris, "The Public Credibility of American Business," *Conference Board Record,* March, 1973, pp. 33–38.
3. Francis X. Sutton, Seymour E. Harris, Carl Kaysen, James Tobin, *The American Business Creed* (N.Y.: Schocken Books, 1956): see especially pp. 354–368.
4. Quoted in Michael Reagan, *The Managed Economy* (N.Y.: Oxford University Press, 1963), p. 124.
5. Sidney Fine, *Laissez Faire and the General Welfare State* (Ann Arbor: University of Michigan Press, 1956, 1964), pp. 103–104.
6. Louis D. Brandeis, *Other People's Money and How the Bankers Use It,* ed. Richard M. Abrams (N.Y.: Harper Torchbooks, pp. vii–xvi).

7. A. A. Berle, Jr. and G. C. Means, *The Modern Corporation and Private Property* (N.Y.: Harcourt Brace & World, 1967), revised edition, p. 8. See Robert J. Larner, *Management Control and the Large Corporation* (N.Y.: Dunellen Publishing Co., 1970) for an update of the Berle-Means study.

8. Quoted in John Tipple (Professor of History, California State University, Los Angeles) *The Capitalist Revolution, A History of American Social Thought 1890–1919* (N.Y.: Pegasus, 1970), p. 18.

9. Quoted in James P. Roche, "Entrepreneurial Liberty and the Fourteenth Amendment," *Labor History,* IV (Winter 1963), p. 31.

10. Quoted by Morrell Heald, Professor of American Studies, Case Western Reserve University, in *The Social Responsibilities of Business: Company and Community, 1900–1960,* The Press of Case Western Reserve University, Cleveland, Ohio, 1970, pp. 29, 32.

11. Walter Lippmann, *Drift and Mastery* (Englewood Cliffs, N.J.: Prentice-Hall, 1961), pp. 22, 23.

12. See Seligman's essay, "The American Corporation: Ideology and Reality," *Dissent,* June 1964. Professor Seligman took this position from the left, but Professor Milton Friedman takes it from the right in *Capitalism and Freedom* (Chicago: University of Chicago Press, 1962), pp. 133–134.

13. A. A. Berle, Jr., *The Twentieth Century Capitalist Revolution* (N.Y.: Harcourt Brace, 1954), p. 188.

14. Robert A. Lively, "The American System," *Business Historical Review,* March 1955, p. 82. Also see Louis Hartz, *Economic Policy and Democratic Thought* (Chicago: Quadrangle, 1948, 1968) and James Willard Hurst, *The Legitimacy of the Business Corporation* (Charlottesville: University Press of Virginia, 1970).

15. Quoted in Reagan, *The Managed Economy,* p. 43.

16. Irving S. Shapiro, "The Adversary System Is the Public Good," *Conference Board Record,* February 1975, p. 10, and Shapiro, "Government and Business," *Vital Speeches,* November 15, 1974, p. 87.

CHAPTER SIX

1. Quoted in Herman E. Kroos, *The Executive Opinion,* (N.Y.: Doubleday & Co., 1970), p. 33.

2. Robert Dahl, *After the Revolution* (New Haven: Yale Fastback, 1970), p. 120.

3. Quoted in Reagan, *The Managed Economy,* p. 122.

4. Henry Manne, "The Myth of Corporate Responsibility, or Will the Real Ralph Nader Please Stand Up?" *Business Lawyer,* Nov. 1970, p. 539.
5. Robert L. Bartley, "Sweden: The Closet Capitalists," *Wall Street Journal,* June 5, 1975, p. 10. For a more extended analysis of Swedish economic policy, see Assar Lindbeck, *Swedish Economic Policy* (Berkeley: University of California Press, 1974).
6. The best overall analyses of the pattern of business-government intervention in Western Europe are Andrew Shonfield, *Modern Capitalism* (N.Y., London: Oxford University Press, 1965) and Raymond Vernon, Ed., *Big Business and the State* (Cambridge: Harvard University Press, 1974).
7. William E. Simon, "Big Government or Freedom—The Case of Economic Freedom Leads to Slavery," *Vital Speeches of the Day,* April 15, 1975, p. 386.
8. William H. Whyte, Jr., *The Organization Man* (N.Y.: Simon and Schuster, 1956).
9. Compton Advertising, Inc., *National Survey on the American Economic System* (The Advertising Council, Inc., Aug. 1975).
10. See Richard Hofstadter, "Whatever Happened to the Antitrust Movement?" in Earl F. Cheit, *The Business Establishment* (N.Y.: Harper & Row, 1964), pp. 113–115, for a discussion of the role of antitrust in American political and economic thought.
11. See S. Perlman, *A History of Trade Unionism in the United States* (N.Y.: The Macmillan Co., 1922).
12. Alexis de Tocqueville, *Democracy in America* (N.Y.: Schocken Books, 4th ed., 1970), Vol. II, p. 167, p. 193.
13. Hannah Arendt, *Men in Dark Times* (N.Y.: Harcourt Brace & World, 1955), pp. 81–82.

CHAPTER SEVEN

1. Herbert Croly, *The Promise of American Life* (N.Y.: E. P. Dutton & Co., 1963), p. 44.
2. Alexis de Tocqueville, *Democracy in America,* Vol. 1, p. 203.
3. Richard Hofstadter, *Social Darwinism in American Life* (Boston: Beacon Press, 1944), p. 55.
4. Edward C. Kirkland, *Dream and Thought in the Business Community* (Chicago: Quadrangle, 1956, 1964), pp. 116–118, 129–130.
5. James Warren Prothro, *The Dollar Decade* (Baton Rouge, La.: State University Press, 1954).

6. See A. Miller, *The Supreme Court and American Capitalism* (N.Y.: Free Press, 1968), pp. 144–45, for a description of "government by contract."
7. The major studies of this phenomenon are Ely Chinoy, *The Automobile Workers and the American Dream* (Boston: Beacon Press, 1955), and Richard Sennett and Jonathan Cobb, *The Hidden Injuries of Class* (N.Y.: Alfred A. Knopf, 1972).
8. John K. Galbraith, *The New Industrial State* (Boston: Houghton Mifflin, 1967), and *Economics and Public Purpose* (Boston: Houghton Mifflin, 1973).
9. Edward S. Mason, "Interests, Ideologies and the Problem of Stability and Growth," *The American Economic Review,* Vol. LIII, No. I, Part I, March 1963, p. 7.
10. Andrew Hacker, "The Elected and the Anointed: Two American Elites," *American Political Science Review,* Sept. 1961, pp. 548–549.
11. Quoted in Herman E. Kroos, *The Executive Opinion* (N.Y.: Doubleday & Co., 1970), p. 5.
12. Walter Lippmann, *A Preface to Morals* (N.Y.: Macmillan, 1929), pp. 66–67.
13. Robert Heilbroner, *The Limits of American Capitalism* (N.Y.: Harper & Row, 1966), pp. 11–12.
14. R. Heilbroner, *ibid.,* pp. 24–25.
15. Thorstein Veblen, *The Engineers and the Price System* (New York: Augustus Kelley, 1963), p. 16; originally published in 1921.
16. *The New Yorker,* Dec. 15, 1975.
17. A. A. Berle, *The Three Faces of Power* (N.Y.: Harcourt Brace & World, 1968), p. 4.
18. Quoted in Justin Kaplan, *Lincoln Steffens: A Biography* (N.Y.: Simon and Schuster, 1974), p. 108.
19. Walter Lippmann, *op. cit.,* p. 188.
20. Letter of Kenneth E. Boulding to Leonard S. Silk, Dec. 11, 1964.
21. Joseph Schumpeter, *Capitalism, Socialism and Democracy* (N.Y.: Harper & Row., 1942), pp. 137–138.

CHAPTER EIGHT

1. *The New York Times,* Dec. 15, 1975, p. 31.
2. Alexander M. Bickel, *The Morality of Consent* (New Haven: Yale University Press, 1975), pp. 119–120.

3. Alexis de Tocqueville, *op. cit.*, II, 130–131.
4. Alfred North Whitehead, *Science and the Modern World:* Lowell Lectures, 1925 (N.Y.: Macmillan, 1946), pp. 287–289.
5. George C. Lodge, *The New American Ideology* (N.Y.: Alfred A. Knopf, 1975).
6. William F. Martin and George Cabot Lodge, "Our Society in 1985—Business May Not Like It," *Harvard Business Review*, Nov.–Dec. 1975, pp. 143–152.
7. Walter Lippmann, *A Preface to Morals* (N.Y.: Macmillan, 1929), pp. 226–227.

Acknowledgments

The authors wish to acknowledge the valuable advice and criticism of the following persons: Alexander B. Trowbridge, G. Clark Thompson, Walter A. Hamilton, Stuart C. Dobson, David G. Moore, Fabian Linden, and Lillian W. Kay of The Conference Board; Sherri Cavan of San Francisco State College; Earl Cheit, Russell Ellis, David Matza, and Michael Rogin of the University of California at Berkeley; Norma Wikler of the University of California at Santa Cruz; Larry Hirschorn of the University of Pennsylvania; Erik Wright of the University of Wisconsin; David Langsam of the Chase Manhattan Bank; Penny Ciancanelli of the New School for Social Research; Mark Silk of Harvard University; Andrew Silk of Haverford College; and John B. Oakes and A. H. Raskin of *The New York Times*. Stephanie Lenway and Sanford Greenberg served as research assistants, and Jean Kidd and Marcie McGaugh typed the manuscript.

We are particularly grateful for the anonymous views expressed by conferees from the following companies:

Allen-Bradley Company
Allied Chemical Corporation
AMAX Inc.
American Cyanamid Company
Ampex Corporation
Amstar Corporation
AMSTED Industries
  Incorporated

249

Aqua-Chem, Inc.
Avery Products Corporation
The Babcock & Wilcox Company
BASF Wyandotte Corporation
The Bechtel Group of
  Companies
Beckman Instruments, Inc.
Bethlehem Steel Corporation
Bliss & Laughlin Industries
  Incorporated
Blount Inc.
Celanese Corporation
Cerro Corporation
The Chesapeake Corporation
  of Virginia
Consolidated-Bathurst Limited
Cummins Engine Company, Inc.
Dana Corporation
Del Monte Corporation
A. B. Dick Company
R. R. Donnelley & Sons
  Company
Dresser Industries, Inc.
E-B Industries, Inc.
Exxon Corporation
Fieldcrest Mills, Inc.
Fluor Corporation
Fuqua Industries, Inc.
General Foods Corporation
Giddings & Lewis, Inc.
The B. F. Goodrich Company
Gulf Oil Corporation
Hammermill Paper Company
Homestake Mining Company
Hughes Tool Company
Ideal Basic Industries, Inc.
International Business Machines
  Corporation

Kerr-McGee Corporation
Koppers Company, Inc.
Kroehler Mfg. Co.
Magma Copper Company
Motorola, Inc.
Oak Industries Inc.
Omark Industries, Inc.
Phillips Petroleum Company
Schlage Lock Company
Sundstrand Corporation and
    Subsidiaries
Texaco Inc.
Textron Inc.
UAL, Inc.
United Aircraft Corporation
United States Steel
    Corporation
Westinghouse Electric
    Corporation
Weyerhaeuser Company

We have sought to quote or describe their views accurately and fairly. But we alone are responsible for the interpretations expressed in this book.

L.S.
D.V.